THE GREATEST COLLECTION

Legends and Lore Behind Hockey's Treasures

Dr. Jeffrey Griffith   Foreword by **Roch Carrier**

The Greatest Collection - Legends and Lore Behind Hockey's Treasures
Dr. Jeffrey Griffith

Content Curation
Griffintown Media in Partnership with the Hockey Hall of Fame

Published in Canada by Griffintown Media Inc.
5548 Saint-Patrick Street, Montreal, QC H4E 1A9
(514) 934-2474 | info@griffintown.com | griffintown.com

All photos were provided from the collections of the Hockey Hall of Fame

ISBN 978-0-9958630-4-0

Copyright © 2019 Griffintown Media Inc.
Text and images reproduced under license by Hockey Hall of Fame. All Rights Reserved.

All Rights Reserved. No part of this publication may be reproduced, stored in a retrieval system, or transmitted, in any form or in any means – by electronic, mechanical, photocopying, recording or otherwise — without prior written permission. All inquiries should be addressed to Griffintown Media Inc.

Printed in Canada by Friesens | Manitoba

PRODUCTION CREDITS

Content Curation
Hockey Hall of Fame
Phil Pritchard
Craig Campbell
Steve Poirier
Izak Westgate

Griffintown Media Inc.
Salma Belhaffaf
Jim McRae

Concept, Design & Production
Griffintown Media Inc.
Jim McRae, President
Salma Belhaffaf, Senior Designer
Jim Hynes, Assistant Editor
Judy Yelon, Proofreader

ON THE COVERS
One of the most precious artifacts in the Hall's collection is an original sweater from the Seattle Metropolitans, winners of the Stanley Cup in 1917 and the first American team to capture the trophy.

*Dedicated to all collectors who seek to support
and celebrate the great sport of hockey.*

TABLE OF CONTENTS

FOREWORD	6
INTRODUCTION	8
CHAPTER 1 PRESERVING HOCKEY'S HERITAGE	10
FEATURED ARTIFACT BILL MOSIENKO LETTER	20
CHAPTER 2 A PRICELESS COLLECTION	22
FEATURED ARTIFACT DANIIL ISAYEV GOALIE MASK	34
CHAPTER 3 GOING PRO	36
FEATURED ARTIFACT GORDIE HOWE SKATES	46
CHAPTER 4 TRAILBLAZERS AND WARRIORS	48
FEATURED ARTIFACT MAURICE RICHARD ORDER OF CANADA	58
CHAPTER 5 PERSONAL TREASURES	60
FEATURED ARTIFACT PUCKS EVOLUTION	76

CHAPTER 6
'THE GOAL WAS ASSISTED BY...' — 78
FEATURED ARTIFACT
DETROIT RED WINGS RUG — 88

CHAPTER 7
THE GLOBAL GAME — 90
FEATURED ARTIFACT
EDINBURGH TROPHY — 102

CHAPTER 8
'BEST GAME YOU CAN NAME' — 104
FEATURED ARTIFACT
SALADA COINS — 114

CHAPTER 9
HOCKEY DETECTIVES — 116
FEATURED ARTIFACT
MARIO LEMIEUX CANADA CUP SWEATER — 132

THE GREATEST COLLECTION BY THE NUMBERS — 134

TUROFSKY — 136

HONOURED GUESTS — 140

BIBLIOGRAPHY — 144

CREDITS — 146

ACKNOWLEDGMENTS — 148

NATIONAL TREASURE SERIES — 150

FOREWORD

On a beautiful day in the summer of 2019, I came across a newspaper article reporting that the National Hockey League was planning to insert microchips in the "jerseys" of its players, and even inside pucks! In a few years, in all 31 NHL rinks, special antennas will gather all kinds of player and game data in real time.

Astonished, amused and very much interested in this bit of news, I couldn't help myself from remembering the time when, at the age of nine or 10, I played hockey back in the little village I was born and grew up in. Back then, no young hockey player would refer to his uniform as a "jersey." It was a "hockey sweater." A "jersey" was a type of fabric the local seamstress turned into light dresses in which the women of the village marched into church to pray on summer Sundays. Back then there were no microchips in our heavy wool hockey sweaters — just like the one on the cover of this book. But there were often mites. Luckily the cold of winter took care of them...for good.

On the village rink, men and boys were proud to wear their wool hockey sweaters. Hockey then was a game for men, and for us future men. The girls who lined the boards had the privilege of witnessing our athletic prowess, and our little on-ice spats, too. Fortunately, girls no longer have to take in the action from the sidelines. And that's one more thing that has changed, for the better, and that you'll learn about in the pages that follow.

We played hockey after school let out in the afternoon. Our rink was in a flat field that was used as a cow pasture in the summer. In winter, it was where a boy could show that, even if he made 18 mistakes in his composition, he knew how to put the puck in the net.

Flipping through the pages of *The Greatest Collection*, I came across the stick used by the great Cyclone Taylor in the early 1900s. That stick, looking not unlike a withered old tree branch, reminded me of the one I played with as a boy. Back then a stick cost about 70 cents. And if most of us could afford one, not everyone could treat himself to a real pair of shin pads. Happily, Dupuis et Frères department store catalogues tucked into our socks were thick enough to absorb the impact of a flying puck.

I was eight years old in 1945, when World War II ended with the bombing of Hiroshima and Nagasaki. Back from the battlefields, accustomed to the discipline of military life and having braved death, some returning soldiers had a tough time adapting to life in our peaceful village. Many of them would lace up their skates on late afternoons and join our hockey games. After spending our days with the pious nuns who taught us in school, we had real admiration for these men who had battled ferocious German warriors. These soldiers wanted to pass along the lessons they had learned overseas to the next generation of boys in our village: the will to win, effort, discipline, teamwork...

A few years later, television appeared in our region. After consulting the local priest, my grandparents decided to buy a TV set. My grandmother explained: "Television is like the radio, except you can see what you hear. I have trouble believing it, but if the priest says it, it must be true", she said.

The next Saturday night, our entire family gathered around the magic box that nobody seemed to know how to even turn on. Suddenly, a miracle! The Montreal Canadiens appeared on the screen! It was as if we were sitting in the Montreal Forum. My grandmother exclaimed: "Me, I say the Devil himself invented this machine."

A few minutes later, the Canadiens scored a goal! A triumphant moment in my grandparents' kitchen. But my grandfather was not happy: "Do me a favour and shut that television off. We can see much better on the radio."

Enough daydreaming. I needed to escape the past and get back to a book project I was working on. My trip to the past had given me a boost of energy! Just like in hockey...straight to the net!

Then the phone rang. "Would you consider writing the foreword to a hockey book, M. Carrier?" a pleasant-sounding young woman asked.

I desperately wanted to say yes, but I was worried that I didn't have the skills for the task at hand. You see, dear reader, I was the worst hockey player in the history of the game. And now

I was being invited to present a book dedicated to the history and evolution of our national game!!! This was exciting! Is life not full of pleasant surprises?

A clumsy player, I spent more time sitting on the bench than darting around the ice. I never once scored a goal, not against a goaltender anyhow. What qualifications do I have to contribute to a book like this one, celebrating some of the most important objects in the history of the game?

It's true that I wrote *The Hockey Sweater*. I even wrote a biography of Maurice Richard, who later presented me with a Canadiens sweater onstage at the Salon du livre book show in Montreal. And I've been given numerous pucks by various hockey teams as I've travelled through their regions. One is even signed by Frank Mahovlich! I have a Jacques Plante hockey card and more than 20 hockey sweaters given to me at readings of *The Hockey Sweater* over the years. I even have a photo of astronaut Robert Thirsk reading it in outer space!

Sitting on the bench, waiting for my turn, which often did not come, I watched my teammates play. It all seemed to come so easily for them. Why couldn't I play that way? I owe a lot to those times when I asked myself: what do I have to do to break out of this cage?

That's when, little by little, I began dreaming about a different kind of goal. Instead of putting the puck in the net, I began to dream of making my pen skate along a sheet of paper. And this dream took me all the way to writing books and being named the National Librarian of Canada in 1997.

In these times of emerging technologies, should we not be improving our service to ordinary citizens? That's what we asked ourselves at the Library. The first step was to gain the support of government ministries, Members of Parliament and other civil servants. But how could one "get the ear" of such busy people?

A member of our team at the time had come across a number of historic hockey photos in our collection, photos taken on outdoor rinks, in cities and small towns, in different eras. He suggested that these photos would make great hockey cards. In meetings and conversations over the years, I'd often heard people say: "It's just like in hockey."

So…let's print up those cards.

And it worked beautifully. The cards ended up opening doors for us at ministries and government offices as we looked for support for our project to update the National Library.

The word "hockey" is a magical one. A few years ago, the illustrator, Sheldon Cohen, and I presented the animated film version of *The Hockey Sweater* to a group of students in Abu Dhabi. After the showing, one of them raised his hand and asked cautiously: "This Maurice Richard, is he your Jesus?" Fair question!

The Greatest Collection will allow you to witness and take part in some of the most exceptional hockey moments created by the people who played the game at all levels, not just in Canada, but all over the world. Who would not be hypnotized by the sight of the pucks Bill Mosienko of the Chicago Black Hawks used to score a record three goals in 21 seconds and not ask themselves: "How did he do it?" Theories will surely be explored, and young players will be inspired to break that record. And some day, one of them will!

Throughout this book, you'll experience special moments that you'll want to live over and over again, and share and discuss them with your children, grandchildren, partners, friends and colleagues. Page after page, photo after photo and paragraph after paragraph, it's a thrilling trip through the history of hockey, and often, the history of our youth!

Still today, as it did with my classmates, the returning soldiers and my family gathered around the TV set all those years ago, hockey continues to bring us together. May it always.

Roch Carrier

THE GREATEST COLLECTION

INTRODUCTION

While it might be a bit of a challenge to live up to a title boasting *The Greatest Collection*, it's made a whole lot easier when the collection in question just happens to represent the greatest game.

Which brings us to this compilation of stories and images that present the deep and rich story of hockey through artifacts — some big, shiny and precious, others small, worn and whose great value is their priceless connection to a great moment or player — all preserved, protected and promoted in perpetuity by the Hockey Hall of Fame.

Since the Hall began producing exhibits in Toronto, the publicly displayed and privately stored collection has formed the cornerstone of the institution's mission to share the history of hockey, the groundwork of which NHL President Clarence Campbell began to lay more than a half century ago. He wrote to Lester Patrick in February 1958 to invite the sport's icon to join the Hall's Selection Committee. "Recently the National Hockey League was invited by the Canadian National Exhibition to lend its endorsement and co-operation in establishing a Hockey Hall of Fame," he shared, "in which the 'heroes' and 'greats' of hockey could be honoured and where their souvenirs and mementoes of various kinds could be placed on display."

Bobby Hewitson, the Hall's first curator, expanded on the vision of telling hockey history through the museum's collection. As he explained to Honoured Member Dan Bain in 1959, "I am always on the lookout for anything in the way of displays... What I am after in addition to old time pictures are famous old trophies or medals, old time equipment such as hockey sticks." The one-man museum guardian requested that Bain, and other fellow legends he knew, contribute to the burgeoning collection.

Over the following six decades, the Hall has built, gathered, displayed and promoted the greatest collection of hockey artifacts in the world. The dream of curators Hewitson and Maurice "Lefty" Reid to provide unparalleled resources to authors and researchers culminated with the dedication of the D.K. (Doc) Seaman Resource Centre in 2009. Artifacts and memorabilia stored in the vast archives can be used to tell hockey history through museum exhibits or travelling displays, or as source materials for articles, books, documentaries and other media. Many important artifacts, the story behind the donations, and their meaning to the staff and visitors to the Hall, add additional significance to the physical objects. To past and present visitors, staff and other interested individuals, the Hall's incomparable collection provides unparalleled insight into the rich history and diversity of the sport.

Rather than narrowly celebrating male-dominated professional achievement, the museum's purpose is to recognize different levels of participation, not solely ice level. In so doing, it desires that the positive values and memories that have shaped communities will be promoted. These efforts reinforce Hewitson's observation to NHL President Campbell. Reflecting on the success of the Hall's luncheon during Hockey Day and Athletic Day at the Canadian National Exhibition on September 5, 1959, at which 31 of the 34 living Honoured Members helped produce one of the institution's most iconic images, he commented, "I do believe that not only did the Hockey Hall of Fame gain much in the way of public goodwill, but that Hockey in general did the same."

"...a Hockey Hall of Fame in which the 'heroes' and 'greats' of hockey could be honoured..."

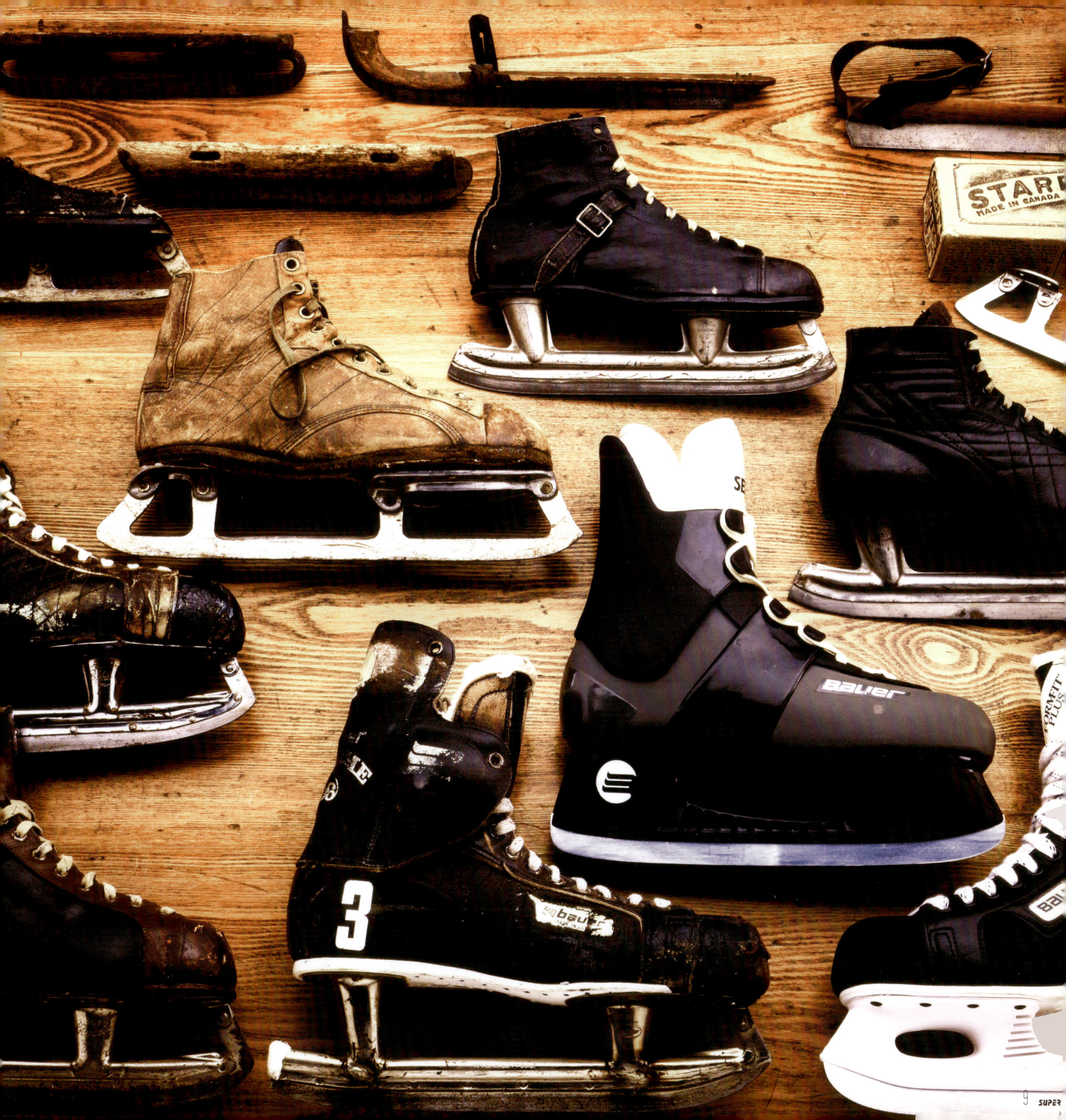
MADE IN CANADA
Bauer
3
9
SUPER

THE GREATEST COLLECTION

CHAPTER 1
PRESERVING HOCKEY'S HERITAGE
From Grassroots to Stained Glass

When Fred "Cyclone" Taylor sent his stick from 1907 to the Hockey Hall of Fame to be stored in "its final resting place" in June 1958, the famous goal-scorer mused in a letter to Curator Bobby Hewitson, "My only hope is that present players and fans will not judge the play of that era by this badly deformed club. They were pressed into shape and after a short period of time would return or try to return to their native state. However, here it is and I hope you will find a place in your building for it."

Taylor's description not only provides a glimpse into the earliest days of hockey, it does so through personal insight and storytelling. It's just one example among thousands that help make the Hall home to hockey's greatest collection, where stories may begin with the artifacts — the greatest collection in the hockey world, in fact — but become complete through the personal connections they make with players and fans alike.

"NIGHBOR DOES NOT DO MUCH LETTER WRITING"
As the Hall began its mission to share the sport's history, the dream of preserving and promoting hockey's role in the community drove its earliest efforts. In September 1958, after the Hall's first display at the Canadian National Exhibition (CNE), Hewitson wrote to NHL President Clarence Campbell how he believed the new museum was "off to a great start" and "we have only scratched the surface of the possibilities the future has in store for us if we stay a safe and sane course."

The first order of business was to assemble images of Honoured Members and data on their careers; easier said than done in an era prior to mass media and instant information retrieval.

In June of '58, Hewitson wrote to *Montreal Star* sports columnist Basil "Baz" O'Meara requesting "if someday — soon — in your [column] — you could ask your readers if some of them might have such pictures of these persons. Perhaps the item might hit the eye of a relative or a good friend of these players and they could help out." The curator specifically requested information on Harry Trihey and Dickie Boon and hoped O'Meara "could suggest that if anyone has such pictures they write me at the Hockey Hall of Fame."

In 1962, after the Selection Committee chose 20 new Honoured Members who were active in the early 20th century, Hewitson fretted about how he was going to acquire so much information in time for preparing public displays. He nervously wrote Campbell sharing that the selection had "imposed a tremendous task for myself in seeking out pictures, stories, etc on each. Just how I will proceed on these I haven't figured out, but I do know I will [need] help from a lot of sources." Hewitson immediately went to work.

On September 10, "Cyclone" Taylor, who "appreciated" Hewitson's problem, sought to share his personal knowledge on Barney Stanley, Riley Hern, Marty Walsh, Harry Cameron and Tom Hooper. After unsuccessfully attempting to gather information regarding Cameron, Hewitson contacted Honoured Member Frank Nighbor but instead heard back from Dave Boehan who explained Nighbor "does not do much letter writing." The curator had to repeat this pattern multiple times in an effort to meet the Hall's mandate. Though the 1962 Hockey Hall of Fame book merely has an insert sharing the names of the 20 new members, Hewitson's tireless efforts enabled him to write citations for each player for the 1963 edition.

Tools of the tree: Early-era scoring sensation Cyclone Taylor worried that future generations would judge him by his branchlike hockey stick.

The almost-a-napkin contract between Cyclone Taylor and the Renfrew Hockey Club for the 1909-10 season was drafted on hotel stationery.

THE GREATEST COLLECTION

Hall artifacts from Bill Mosienko's record hat trick include the three pucks and game ticket from Madison Square Garden.

The Golden Goal display from the 2010 Olympics is a fan favourite, with the wayward puck front and centre.

A HAT — AND POCKET — TRICK

It's amazing to consider that among all the artifacts shiny and bright in the Hall's collection, a few humble hockey pucks are counted amongst the most prized possessions — and most popular.

On March 23, 1952, Bill Mosienko accomplished one of the most unusual and unbeatable feats in hockey history. Over 21 short seconds, the career Black Hawk forward scored three times against the New York Rangers, a record unlikely to be beaten. Interestingly, Mosienko achieved a similar feat a decade earlier when he scored his first two NHL career goals — also 21 seconds apart. The Mosienko moment will forever be remembered by fans thanks to the Hall display featuring the Lady Byng winner's stick from the famous game, along with the trio of pucks, of course. The display is one of the first that visitors come across when entering the Hall.

Six decades later, Sidney Crosby achieved immortality of his own, but this time in a split second. His dramatic Golden Goal to clinch the 2010 Olympic gold medal for Canada in overtime against the United States touched off a celebration for the ages, and instantly became an iconic hockey moment.

The Hall's efforts to collect Crosby's equipment for posterity were no less Olympian.

One of the game's linesmen, for example, unwittingly picked up the instantly-famous puck and put it in his pocket, later to return it to the International Ice Hockey Federation's offices in Zurich; IIHF President René Fasel himself would deliver it to the Hall. One of Crosby's gloves landed in the netting behind the goal and had to be retrieved from a fan. Another glove inadvertently ended up in a teammate's equipment bag. The stick also temporarily disappeared with rumours, innuendo and conspiracy flying like Sid the Kid's discarded gear during the goal celebration, before finding its way to the Hall. Today, the Golden Goal display unites all of the key pieces, along with the net from the game, connecting fans to a moment that will live forever.

CHAPTER 1 | PRESERVING HOCKEY'S HERITAGE

Alexander Ovechkin's game-used skates from the 2018-19 season are among the Hall's most recent artifacts. A closer look at the skates reveals the name of the superstar's son.

To: Phil
Ovie scored 50th goal with these!
Brock

LATEST GREATEST

As much as the Hall's curation team has always been ready to spring into action when a great moment occurs — ever on the lookout to mark the occasion with a game or personal artifact — it also keeps abreast of impending milestones and reaches out to players and teams with the goals of honouring the individual, recognizing the achievement and growing the collection.

And that's exactly how Alexander Ovechkin's skates ended up on Phil Pritchard's desk at the Resource Centre one day following the 2019 season.

The Hall's curator reached out to Washington Capitals' Equipment Manager, Brock Myles, mentioning that Ovechkin's 1,200-career-point milestone was certainly worth commemorating, as was his 51-goal performance to lead the NHL in '19 and earn yet another Rocket Richard Trophy. Myles agreed, and a few weeks later a special package arrived in the mail — the contents of which left no doubt as to the owner. (The yellow laces give it away.)

The skates will no doubt make it into an exhibit of the future Hall of Famer one day for all to enjoy.

It should be noted that Ovechkin counts himself among the Hall's many fans, finding himself in awe of its artifacts. During one visit to the Resource Centre, he took one of Maurice Richard's sticks from the giant stick rack and was amazed to hold it, handle it and basically wondered how the Rocket could score so many goals with it: It was so heavy, the blade was straight...and "can I keep it?!"

It's just another example of the connection hockey's greatest collection makes with hockey's great fans.

THE GREATEST COLLECTION

Hall of Fame artifacts like Johnny Bower's chest protector, which he favoured for virtually his entire legendary career, leave visitors wondering about the rudimentary equipment worn by players from earlier eras — especially those paid to stop the puck!

Hewitson appreciated the assistance he received, offering his thanks to Honoured Member Frank Smith in September '62. "It is only with this cooperation that the success of the Hall can be achieved." Likewise, when the Hall's second curator Maurice "Lefty" Reid wrote to George Armstrong to inform the former Maple Leaf of his enshrinement, he asked "do you have one or more items of personal significance that you would be willing to loan or donate to the Hall for display? If so, I would be pleased to obtain it and incorporate it into a display." Both early curators recognized the importance of the museum's members themselves in building the collection as well as adding new voices to the narrative.

A SMALL DUPLICATING MACHINE

Hewitson would build on the groundwork he laid by creating a resource library to be "used by newspaper writers, radio and TV persons, who might be looking for interesting old time stories, incidents, dates, etc." Requests were so frequent, Lefty Reid told the NHL's Campbell in October 1968, that he wanted to acquire "a small duplicating machine" in order to fulfill the "steady correspondence from persons wishing background information on members and other hockey data."

The demand for such information about hockey greats and the game itself would prove insatiable in the years after the move to BCE Place (Brookfield Place) in downtown Toronto. The Hall had new opportunities to grow, preserve and share information contained in its library. John Armstrong describes the Hockey Hall of Fame Resource Centre and Archives' "purpose" in the 1993 HHOF *Yearbook* as aspiring "to collect, organize and preserve any type of documentation related to hockey." Acquisition efforts for over three decades had resulted in the "world's largest collection of scrapbooks, periodicals, books, programs and guides on hockey, the centre even includes hockey cards, schedules and ticket stubs." This explosion in material quickly became untenable to store and a specialized facility would be needed.

CHAPTER 1 | PRESERVING HOCKEY'S HERITAGE

GREAT COLLECTION

The Hall's D.K. (Doc) Seaman Hockey Resource Centre is a special place. Opened in 2009 and residing in 18,000 square feet of custom designed, secure and temperature-controlled archive in the west end of Toronto, the Resource Centre and Archives serves thousands of correspondents, media, teams, authors, filmmakers, teachers and students. The Resource Centre's holdings boast an astonishing 26,000 published hockey books, programs and guides; approximately 20,000 individual player, team, league and trophy files; over 450 binders of hockey cards, team photos, tickets and schedules; 750 glass negatives, 4,000 film reels, 32,000 photos, 500,000 digital images and 1,000,000 photo negatives. The facility also houses more than 4,000 historical sticks — in the biggest and most fascinating stick rack in the world — and countless other game-worn artifacts. Heaven for any hockey fan.

TIME CAPSULE STUFF

The Hall often builds its collection through direct donations, unsolicited contributions and procurement after significant moments and milestones. As it solidified its position as a museum and storehouse, it enhanced its reputation in the eyes of donors who began to recognize the institution as a safe and permanent custodian for their piece of history. Rather than simply loaning an item and anticipating its return, donors would come to see the Hall as the ultimate destination and rightful home for many of hockey's most significant artifacts.

It all began with Hewitson's tireless efforts to obtain images and information on Honoured Members, and ambitiously seeking to acquire physical artifacts to put on display. In June 1958, he wrote to Honoured Member William Northey that "Cyclone Taylor is sending me an old stick which he used in his early days of action and Percy LeSueur (now in Hamilton) is sending me an old goalkeeper's stick."

While players willingly entrusted their mementoes and memories to the Hall, other donors needed some convincing. Hewitson sought to acquire the O'Brien Trophy, an elegant award that had been awarded to the National Hockey Association's champion beginning in 1910 and to various National Hockey League clubs through 1950. J. Ambrose O'Brien agreed to send his namesake award for the '58 CNE if it would protect and insure his property. He later decided to permanently store the artifact once the museum earned legal incorporation and he could transfer title to the institution. Despite these complexities, the addition of the O'Brien Trophy relates an important part of hockey history, one that extends across decades and leagues. O'Brien himself would become an Honoured Member (1962) with his image residing under the famed stained glass of the Great Hall.

The O'Brien Trophy is one of the most elegant artifacts in the Hall's collection.

15

THE GREATEST COLLECTION

Dickie Boon retired from playing in 1905, but went on to manage the Wanderers until 1916, winning the Stanley Cup four times along the way. He's shown in the photo above, second row, seated *(left)*, wearing suit and tie.

CHAPTER 1 | PRESERVING HOCKEY'S HERITAGE

A boon to the collection were the skates used by Hall of Famer Dickie Boon more than 100 years ago as player with the Montreal Wanderers.

THE GREATEST COLLECTION

In addition to deliberate attempts to acquire pieces of hockey history, there is the odd occasion when the Hall receives unsolicited, unexpected, yet priceless treasures, something Phil Pritchard, Vice President, Resource Centre and Curator, a.k.a. "Keeper of the Cup," calls rare but "amazing and always exciting." Such was the case in 1993 when Mrs. Doris Cox, the daughter of Billy Barlow (a member of the Montreal Amateur Athletic Association from 1893-97), approached the Hall to donate some of her father's hockey memorabilia, which included an 1893 Stanley Cup ring, the first year in which the great trophy was awarded. Mrs. Cox hoped the donation would assist "the players on those early teams [being] recognized for what they started." Her amazing gesture, along with the tradition started in 2007 by the Anaheim Ducks to donate a team ring each season, means the Hall's Stanley Cup ring collection now spans 125 years.

Whether seeking out an important artifact, or being surprised by an unexpected donation, the Hall holds dear signature items from the sport's earliest figures, mostly lone examples of a player's contribution. In the instance of Honoured Member Dickie Boon, however, the museum has two. Remarkably, the staff received two different pairs of skates donated almost five decades apart.

Hoard of the Rings: The Billy Barlow donation was the first Stanley Cup ring donated to the Hall. Cup ring donations have become a tradition. Barlow is shown far right, seated.

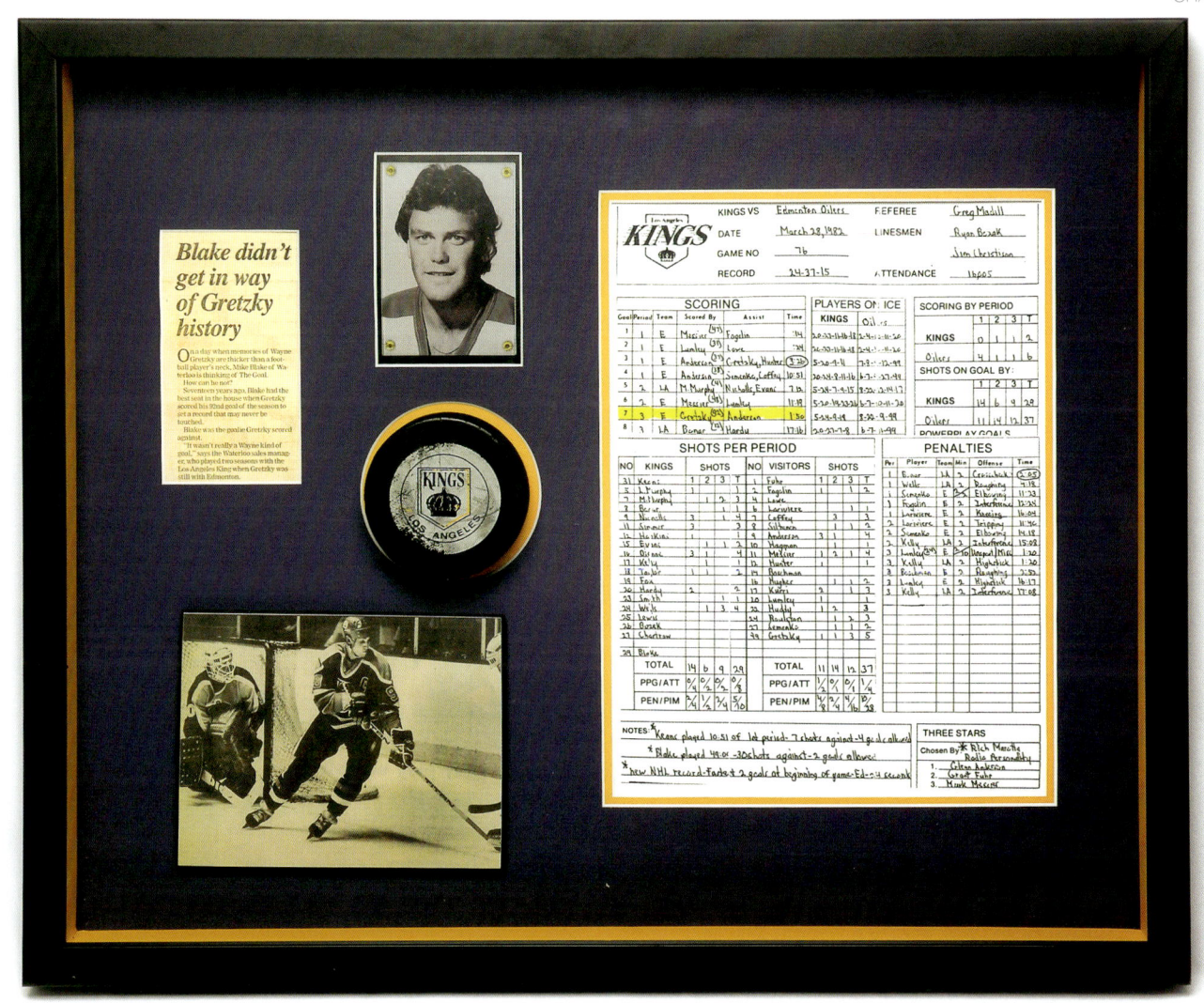

Boxscore: The framed game account, and puck, from Gretzky's record night was obtained from Mike Blake through the Hall's outreach program.

99'S 92ND AND OTHER GREAT OUTREACH

Mike Blake may not have been inducted into the Hall like his famous uncle, Toe, or the player who scored on him while he was playing goal for the Los Angeles Kings on March 28, 1982, but he has left his mark on the collection. The goal he allowed was Wayne Gretzky's 92nd, and last, of his record-exploding 1981-82 season. Gretzky's Oilers had two games left in the season and everyone thought he would score again, but he didn't, making the puck and scoresheet from the Kings game instant and coveted artifacts to add to the Hall's collection, which Blake had framed and eventually donated.

"Allowing that goal was my greatest claim to fame," he said with a laugh.

Blake played a total of 40 NHL games over parts of three seasons, all with the Kings, injuries limiting his career.

Today, the Hall is proactive in its outreach to grow the collection, including working closely with new inductees to identify artifacts that celebrate the individual's career and share further insight into the game. Upon the announcement from the Selection Committee of a new Honoured Member, Hall staff will pay a visit to the inductee and his or her family and discuss the donations that will become part of the collection. It's a very personal approach and an elegant touch that sets the Hall apart.

These efforts continually build on Hewitson's observation to Clarence Campbell in June 1958 just as the Hall was about to open its first public exhibit in Toronto. As he surveyed the initial efforts to amass a collection and build the inaugural exhibits, the curator reflected on how "we are not letting any grass grow under our feet. If there is something [missing] when the Hall opens it won't be because we didn't try."

"Allowing that goal was my greatest claim to fame."

FEATURED ARTIFACT

FEW HALL ARTIFACTS GIVE INSIGHT INTO A FAMOUS EVENT WITH MORE CLARITY THAN A DONATION RECEIVED IN THE SUMMER OF 2019.

THE TYPE-WRITTEN AND SIGNED LETTER WAS A CORRESPONDENCE BETWEEN BILL MOSIENKO AND A FAN, EXPLAINING HOW THE CHICAGO BLACK HAWKS FORWARD MANAGED TO SCORE A HAT TRICK IN A RECORD 21 SECONDS AGAINST THE NEW YORK RANGERS IN 1952.

MOSIENKO'S RECORD NIGHT GENERATED FIVE PRICELESS ARTIFACTS FOR THE COLLECTION: 3 PUCKS, 1 STICK AND NOW THE LETTER — ALMOST 60 YEARS ON.

389 Cathedral Ave.
Winnipeg Manitoba
R2x 1J1

Dear David:
Thank you for your most welcome letter.
You asked about the Pony Line. Playing with Max and Doug Bentley. I was the right winger on that line, with Max centering and Doug playing left wing. We were light weights with me being the heavyweight at 165 lbs. Our speed and movement of the puck to the one ahead was our big asset and knowing one anothers moves made it a thrill to play as a line.

We played to the largest crowd in N.H.L. history (in those days) of 20,008 fans. Biggest mistake was of management breaking up our line.

My theory in hockey was to play the game as it should be played, good tough body contact if necessary, Not as todays hockey with interference, hooking and grabbing. I had tremendous speed and used it to an advantage letting the other player try to stop or catch up to me, ending up with them getting the penalties. I was built solid and would never back down from any unnecessary roughness. That is why I never had to many penalties assessed against me through my career.

The record of scoring 3 goals in 21 seconds in New York against the New York Rangers on March 23rd. 1952 was no doubt a thrill that I will always remember. I have been asked about it many times and it seems as though I have a photo memory of the actions that took place and of the players.

Prior to scoring the 3 goals, Lorne Anderson had beaten me on at least 3 occasions which I thought should have been goals. When the opportunity came in the 3rd. period, receiving a pass from my centreman Gus Bodnar, I went around this defenseman and coming in on Anderson decided to put the puck on the ice to his right side, knowing that he would not be able to reach it with his glove etc. That goal was scored at 6.09 which was my 29th. goal of the season. I retrieved that puck and asked my coach Ebbie Goodfellow to hold on to it for me.

We faced off again and Bodnar was able to get the puck to me on right wing, was able to stickhandle around the checking wingman and once again around the same defenseman, coming in on the goalie I decided to put it in the same place as the last one. This was at 6.20 . That was my 30th. goal which was quite a feat in those days. Retrieved the puck and asked the coach not to worry about the other puck as this is the one I really wanted.

The puck was faced off and once again Bodnar got the face-off and passed it over to George Gee the left winger, he was able to avoid his check and relayed the puck to me, was able to get around the same defenseman again, coming in on the goalie I felt that he would play me for the same shot, instead, I decided to pull him out of the net and put it up high to his right.
That was at 6.30 .

2

Never paid to much attention to this goal even though it was a "Hat Trick" until one of our players, Jim Peters hollered to me to get the puck because it was a record. Did retrieve that puck and handed it to the coach to hold for me.

The 3 pucks and my hockey stick are in the HOCKEY HALL OF FAME in Toronto.

Gus Bodnar asssissted on all 3 goals.
I believe this is what you wanted to hear from me.
Things just happened so quickly.
Thanking you once again for your letter.

Sincerely,
Bill Mosienko

THE GREATEST COLLECTION

CHAPTER 2
A PRICELESS COLLECTION
Spanning Three Centuries

It's common knowledge Stanley Cup-winning teams are given time with the trophy so players and coaches can each enjoy it with family and friends. It's a wonderful tradition that began after the New Jersey Devils won their first Stanley Cup in 1995. It's also commonly known that to the victors go the spoils only for a little while, typically during the summer months when the Cup travels to hometowns, barbecues and even mountaintops. The silver chalice is returned to its permanent home at the Hockey Hall of Fame soon after the last celebration and the pursuit of its temporary ownership starts again the following season.

The 1961 Chicago Black Hawks were a bit more Cup clingy.

When they won the Cup that year, the Hawks were so intent on keeping it that management built a display at the Chicago Stadium so fans could enjoy it. It would take an intervention by Hall Curator Bobby Hewitson who convinced the Hawks that the Cup was such a popular draw at the museum that it should remain in its rightful home. It was agreed, and the famous trophy remains the greatest treasure in the Greatest Collection to this day.

To be sure, not all artifacts at the Hall hold the same allure as the Stanley Cup, but there are aspects of history, achievement and continuity in each piece in its vast collection. It didn't happen by accident.

The Hall explicitly chronicles the evolution of the sport across three centuries. Hewitson described the shrine's vast aspirations for telling the complex history of hockey when he wrote to NHL President Clarence Campbell on February 14, 1958. He wanted to gather information and artifacts regarding the "early history in Kingston, Halifax, Montreal and elsewhere, when teams with limited players started,

The Stanley Cup was the focus of a Black Hawks tribute at the Morris B. Sachs department store in Chicago in April 1961.

22

When Queen's was king: The Queen's University Golden Gaels from Kingston, ON, Canada, who played in the Inter-Provincial Amateur Hockey Union, and won the Allan Cup in 1909 and twice in 1910 (challenges). Jock Harty, with beard and fur hat, was the coach.

THE GREATEST COLLECTION

when six men hockey replaced seven men, the history of the goal nets up to the present style, something on hockey sticks of the early days, [and] a review of the changing rules." The Hall's collection connects visitors to these changes and transitions in play, equipment and milestones that have shaped the game.

"VERY OLD" EQUIPMENT

Visitors are often amazed at the perceived primitiveness and the extreme usage of old equipment. These artifacts show the impact of a physical game that has steadily increased in speed and intensity. The Hall's collection relates this development. As the Hall prepared its first public exhibits in Toronto, Campbell sent Hewitson an intriguing artifact. Writing on August 8, 1958, the NHL President informed the curator that he was sending a "very old pair of home made skates. They are made out of wood carved to the proper shape and the skates themselves are made from old files which have been smoothed down. You will note that there are holes for straps and in your exhibit you should, perhaps, provide something in the nature of straps to indicate how they would be put on." Campbell hoped that these artifacts would show the origin of hockey and serve as an early example of equipment.

While some individuals made homemade equipment like skates, once professional hockey emerged, gear needed to be able to survive persistent use. Percy LeSueur, goaltending star of the pre-NHL Ottawa Senators, gave his game-used stick in one of the shrine's earliest artifact donations. This mass of wood has remained a favourite of Hockey Hall of Fame staff for decades. On the stick, LeSueur etched dates into the wood to signify when he used the tool. This period-specific wood-burning on the stick, the achievements he accomplished with the piece of equipment such as early Stanley Cup victories and an early form of an all-star game, as well as the fact that the Hall has photo matched the artifact has made the hunk of lumber one of the most important early-20th-century artifacts in the collection.

Percy LeSueur displays the elegance of early-era hockey in this classic card from his days with the Ottawa Senators. A closeup of his goaltending stick shows his name stamped into the wooden shaft.

CHAPTER 2 | A PRICELESS COLLECTION

Ahead of the curve. Teammates Stan Mikita and Bobby Hull were early adopters of the — really — curved stick.

Goaltending sticks, especially vintage pieces when players switched equipment fewer times than modern athletes, bear the marks of chronic use and the passions of gameplay. A stick used by John Ross Roach during the 1922 playoffs after his rookie season, in which he and the Toronto St. Patricks won the Stanley Cup, bears the scars of extensive use and battles. The Hall's collection sometimes hints at subtle changes in how players participated in the game. Other times, however, the changes are stunning and shocking, as is the case with Stan Mikita's and Bobby Hull's remarkable curves on their sticks, which helped their shots, and careers, take flight. Whereas many sticks had a straight blade, the purposeful modifications by the Chicago Black Hawk stars in the late 1960s resulted in the game dramatically quickening and becoming more dangerous for goaltenders.

REACHING MILESTONES

Artifacts serve as important mementoes that can commemorate a specific accomplishment. While team milestones are important markers of success, many artifacts in the Hall's collection celebrate individual accomplishment. The standard of excellence, however, has evolved over the previous six decades. Even before the Hall moved to Toronto, Frank Selke wrote to Hewitson regarding efforts to start the Canadian Sports Hall of Fame at the Canadian National Exhibition. As he shared on August 12, 1955, "for some time I have been gathering hockey sticks which were actually used by players when they scored their two-hundredth goals. I also have additional sticks used by Maurice Richard when he passed some famous milestones in his career, as well as the stick used by Ace Bailey the night he was so badly hurt at Boston." Rather than sending these items to support the flailing efforts in Kingston, the Montreal executive offered the historical pieces to the Sports Hall until the Hockey Hall of Fame became a more permanent institution.

25

THE GREATEST COLLECTION

The photo of John Ross Roach *(above)* shows him with what would become a prized Hall artifact, his well-used goalie stick *(right)*.

CHAPTER 2 | A PRICELESS COLLECTION

That *nuit* in Toronto: Maurice Richard holds the milestone puck from his 324th NHL regular-season goal that tied him with Nels Stewart on the all-time regular season scoring list. The goal, and photo, were shot on October 29, 1952, at Maple Leaf Gardens.

Nels Stewart was a star player with the Montreal Maroons and held the career NHL regular-season goal record until being surpassed by Rocket Richard. This photo was taken no later than the 1927-28 NHL season.

27

THE GREATEST COLLECTION

A collection of 200-goal hockey sticks was an early star attraction at the Hall.

You score 802 goals in your NHL career, you get a full display at the Hall of Fame. It's a rule. Wayne Gretzky's stick, gloves, helmet, the Kings puck for goal 802, even the game net form one of the most popular attractions at the Hall.

Implicit in Selke's proposal was that 200 goals represented the pinnacle of personal achievement. When the Hall's program of 1962 displayed a picture of the stick display, 21 players had achieved the milestone. This exhibit of milestone sticks permitted the Hall to add to its collection as history unfolded. For example, as Red Kelly, Andy Bathgate and Alex Delvecchio all inched closer to scoring their 200th career goal, Hewitson informed Campbell on December 15, 1961, and December 26, 1961, that he had requested the sticks for the Hall's display. As scoring increased, however, this initial standard became too common.

As Hewitson nervously wrote to Campbell on March 23, 1964, one side of the double panel display had been filled and the Hall still had "five new sticks to display and thus will need to start on the other side of the double panel if the present idea is carried out." The curator suggested raising the standard to 250 goals, but the NHL president initially scoffed at the idea. Ultimately, however, too many players reached the milestone and the Hall had to adjust how it considered individual achievement and displayed the accomplishment. By 1969 when Lefty Reid published the first Hall program in the *Hockey's Heritage* format, he showed that 54 players had reached at least 200 career goals. When the second curator issued the final edition of *Hockey's Heritage* in 1982, goal production had exploded and 43 players had a minimum of 300 career goals. By the end of the 2018-19 regular season, 45 players have scored at least 500 goals in their careers. Because of this ever-increasing production, the Hall has had to adjust how it displays achievement while balancing era-specific accomplishment against more modern expectations.

On March 23, 1994, coincidentally exactly 30 years after Hewitson wrote to Campbell recognizing that the Hall's initial measure of success was beginning to be exceeded, Wayne Gretzky passed Gordie Howe as the all-time goal scorer in NHL history when he scored his 802nd goal. The Hall created an iconic display to match the splendour of its new exhibitions at BCE Place (now Brookfield Place). Initially, the Hall acquired the puck, stick, gloves and helmet that Gretzky used during that game and later obtained the net from the Great Western Forum in Los Angeles. This large exhibit of artifacts confronts visitors with a virtually complete assortment of mementoes that established one of hockey's most prestigious milestones.

Solid Syl Apps hands Leafs' General Manager Frank Selke a classic straight blade stick at Maple Leaf Gardens.

A GREAT ERROR

Of all the interesting pieces in the Hockey Hall of Fame's collection of Wayne Gretzky artifacts — and they have lots — perhaps the most curious, and humorous, is one based on a mistake.

On October 30, 1997, The Great One wore an alternate New York Rangers navy blue Liberty jersey in a game against the New York Islanders. Fans were no doubt anticipating Gretzky's visit to Long Island, even if he was representing the regional rivals, but perhaps less prepared for the noticeable error stitched above his iconic 99.

Instead of the correct spelling of the world's most famous hockey name, the letters G-R-E-T-K-Z-Y somehow slipped by everyone's attention and made it onto the game jersey of the game's greatest. The Rangers would lose to the Islanders 5-3, and although Gretzky would record just one assist on the night his name was correctly entered on the scoresheet.

For its part, the Hall saw the mistake as an opportunity to add the piece to its collection of Gretzky material in a good-natured way. So among all the impressive milestone artifacts and honours that surround the most celebrated hockey career of all time, there hangs a funny reminder that even hockey royalty can be prone to the odd oversight.

It also helps reinforce the human quality behind the Hall's collection.

CHAPTER 2 | A PRICELESS COLLECTION

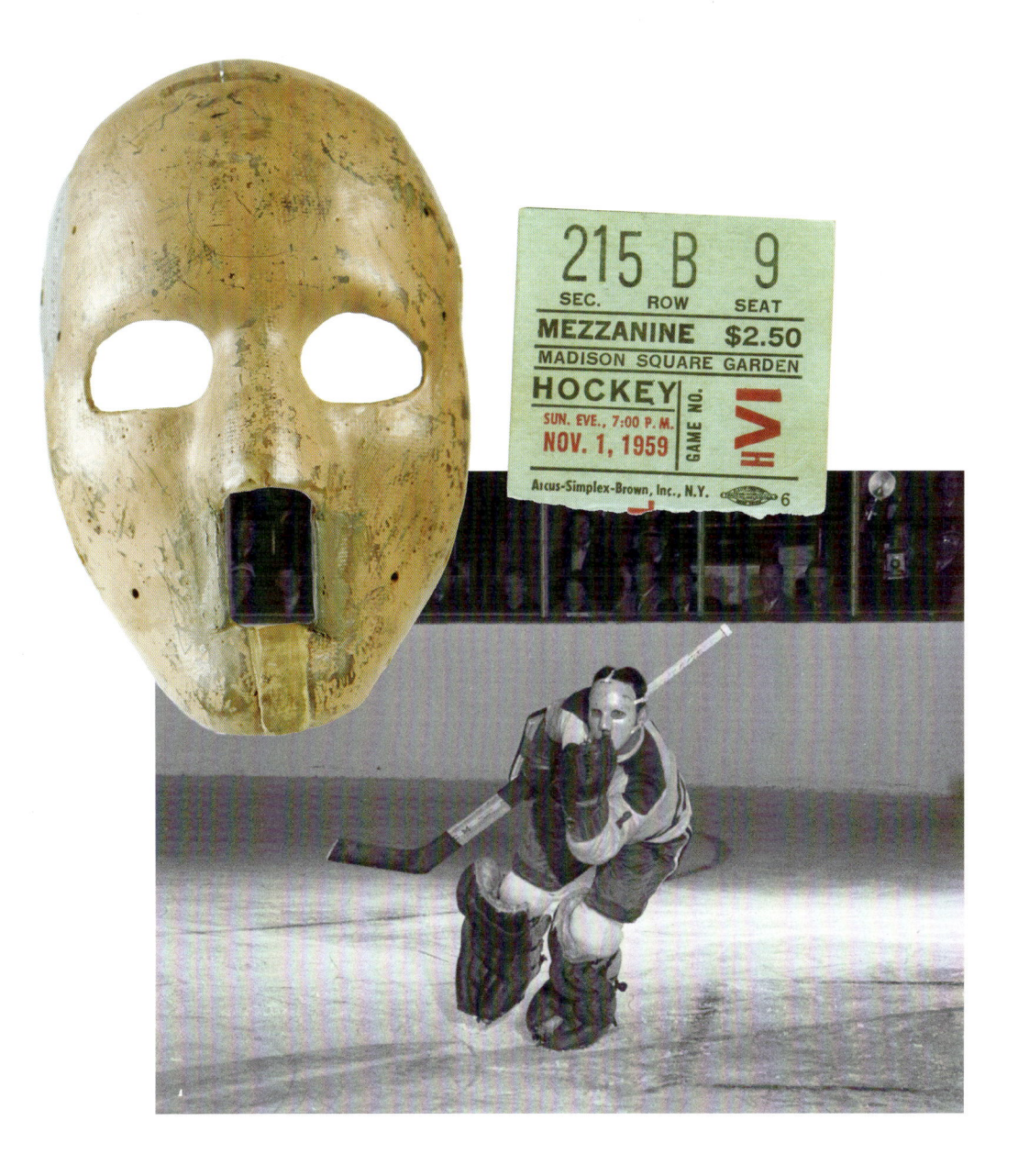

Jacques Plante was the first regular NHL masked-minder, while Andy Brown was the last maskless hold-out — but only during games: He wore a mask in practice during his career. The mask and ticket stub from the famous debut is shown at left.

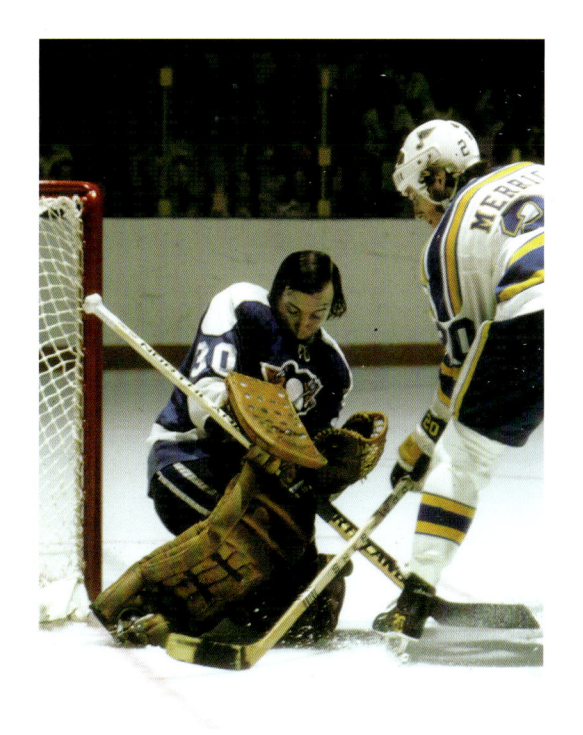

SAVING FACE

Consider the game of hockey from the ice up and it's hard to conceive that the last piece of equipment conceived, really, was facial protection. Skates were a given, given the nature of motive power required, as were sticks, of course, and then shin pads and goalie pads. Check. Check. Check. Why it took so long to even consider a goalie mask is a bit of a curiosity, especially that they were made to protect against the missed aim of the only real target in the game, the net, which was itself safeguarded by the goalie.

The truth is that the mask was a relatively early invention, the first real mask, rudimentary as it was, was introduced in 1930, in fact. Its widespread adoption would be slow, however, owing to limitations in technology, peer pressure — it was long felt that a goalie would be less courageous if he faced game action with anything other than his face — and marketing: The story went that team owners and managers wanted fans to be able to see their heroes' full image as they fronted the net. Whatever the reason, it took the legendary Jacques Plante to break the mould by wearing the first protective mask in an NHL game in 1959. It was a game-changing moment.

The goaltender fraternity was quick to follow Plante's lead, and by the early 1970s masks were accepted as standard goal line equipment, with the Pittsburgh Penguins' Andy Brown being the lone bald-face outlier in 1974. And goalies being goalies, the mask would soon take on a whole separate aura with the advent of artwork designed to express individual personalities or themes. And a good thing, too.

Mask art has become the greatest self-expression in all of professional sport, connecting goalies with fans through commonly shared imagery and imagination. The Hockey Hall of Fame is a prime beneficiary of the art movement, having amassed the most extensive and eclectic display of goalie masks in the world, in the process creating one of the most popular displays for fans visiting the museum.

THE GREATEST COLLECTION

Some of the NHL's major trophies are the biggest draw at the Hall, and probably always will be. They are: Lady Byng Memorial Trophy, the Presidents' Trophy, the Hart Memorial Trophy, the Vezina Trophy, the Conn Smythe Trophy, the Prince of Wales Trophy, the Stanley Cup, the Frank J. Selke Trophy, the James Norris Memorial Trophy.

"THE HOME OF THE STANLEY CUP"

The Hall's extensive collection of trophies from both the amateur and professional ranks is well documented and among the most popular exhibits for visitors. Today, the eloquent and reverential displays in the former Bank of Montreal building and throughout the display floors speak to the legacy, importance and status of these prizes to both the sport and the Hall. However, while Hewitson immediately recognized the desire of visitors to interact with and examine these awards, initially the Hall could only temporarily display the NHL trophies. The close association between the museum's reputation as the repository of hockey's greatest awards and visitors' ability to intimately connect to these prizes is a key motivator in the Hall's effort to share its collection with hockey fans.

Questions over where the Stanley Cup could be displayed emerged once the Hall opened its building at the CNE. As the NHL's Campbell wrote to Hewitson on December 12, 1961, regarding the aforementioned *affaire* Hawks: "as you know, the Chicago Team were the winners of the Stanley Cup and they went to some trouble and expense to create a display area for it in the foyer in the Stadium and it has been a matter of considerable interest and curiosity and naturally they would like to get it back." Three days later, Hewitson regretfully wrote, "I will see that the Cup is delivered to Maple Leaf Gardens on January 6 as you suggest so they may take it back to Chicago. I am sorry it will be going because everyone who comes into the Hall looks for it almost the first thing." Even from the earliest days of the museum, the Stanley Cup has been the central artifact for the Hall.

The Hall's extensive collection of trophies...is well documented and among the most popular exhibits for visitors.

THE HALL'S GREAT HALL

Today, the Esso Great Hall in the majestic former Bank of Montreal building houses all of the NHL trophies year-round. As visitors walk up the marble stairs to the beautiful 19th-century edifice, they are immediately surrounded by an august environment celebrating sport and urban growth. Each trophy has its own case and placard detailing the history of the award. The star attraction, and centre of attention, is the Stanley Cup, openly displayed so guests can take a photo, examine and touch the beloved trophy that has shaped hockey competition across three centuries.

Additionally, dozens of non-NHL trophies dot the Hall's exhibitions. These include current and historic awards such as the Bank Mercantile trophies, John Ross Robertson Cups, the Memorial Cup and the Allan Cup. Each of these prizes has its own history, personality and legacy in shaping hockey history.

HALL AND LOBBY

Hewitson eventually lobbied for a change in policy that would permit the Hall to become the permanent home for the NHL trophies except for presentation events. As he wrote Campbell on May 10, 1962, visitors continually yearned to connect to the Stanley Cup, resulting in the curator desiring that either "originals or replicas of all trophies" be stored "in the Hall at all times." Fortunately, the Hall did not have a gaping absence in its exhibits when the league required the awards but rather temporarily replaced the trophies with other artifacts from its collection. As Hewitson noted on November 14, 1962, once he learned the Vezina Trophy, Calder Memorial Trophy, Prince of Wales Trophy and the Hart Trophy were returning to the Hall, "I will arrange at once to have all Trophies received placed in the Trophy Case, and will remove the Sweaters presently occupying that space." Fortunately, the NHL eventually mandated that the trophies could remain and have a permanent presence in the Hall, allowing the museum to make these popular artifacts a central feature of its exhibition.

FEATURED ARTIFACT

HOCKEY FANS LOVE GOALIES. THEY MIGHT LOVE GOALIE MASKS MORE. THE ART, THE SELF-EXPRESSION, THE COOL FACTOR HELP MAKE GOALIE MASKS THE MOST UNIQUE PROTECTIVE EQUIPMENT IN ALL OF TEAM SPORTS. THE HALL'S COLLECTION OF MASKS IS WORLD FAMOUS AND ONE OF THE MOST POPULAR EXHIBITS AT THE MUSEUM.

THE MASK OF TEAM RUSSIA'S DANIIL ISAYEV FROM THE 2018 IIHF U18 WORLD CHAMPIONSHIP MAY NEVER MAKE IT INTO THE MUCH-VISITED DISPLAY, BUT THE PHOTO OF IT FROM ARCHIVES, RICH RED WITH RUSSIAN HERALDRY JUXTAPOSED AGAINST SHOOTOUT ICE FOLLOWING AN OVERTIME WIN AGAINST SLOVAKIA, IS WORTHY OF THE HERMITAGE, LET ALONE THE HALL.

35

THE GREATEST COLLECTION

CHAPTER 3
GOING PRO

The Hall's Big-Big-League Artifacts

The Hockey Hall of Fame's collection transforms the sport's history from still photographs and grainy video into vibrant colour and powerful detail. Whereas fans can often only associate with individuals from the earliest eras of hockey history through black and white images, interacting with the shrine's collection brings depth, dimension and nuance to how players participated in the sport. The rise of professional hockey created distinct identities and fan bases to connect to the sport.

Whether through current or defunct teams or through an examination of a legend's career, artifacts in the Hall's collection span the complete history of the game from its origins more than a century ago to its present-day popularity, especially at the professional level. From the earliest, heavy wool sweaters to state-of-the-art, super-light fabrics scientifically designed to improve performance, the displays showcase the evolution of equipment like jerseys, but, almost more importantly, resonate with fans who invariably have a connection with a hometown or favourite team, logo or number. (Nines and 99s are among the most popular.)

FROM ASSOCIATION TO LEAGUE

A white wool sweater with a bold red stripe and well-worn "W" patch from the early 20th century, among the Hall's oldest artifacts, celebrates the emergence of professional hockey in one of Canada's most important cities. Though the

Early sweaters are fan-favourites at hockey's Hall, including the ancient artifacts and photos from Montreal Wanderers and the Seattle Metropolitans.

Canadiens have played for over a century, fans are often less aware of the Wanderers who competed alongside Montreal's current team in the National Hockey Association. The artifact silently attests to a lost franchise that transitioned from an amateur group to one of the most successful early professional teams.

The Hall's Wanderers sweater belonged to the team's captain, Cecil Blachford. A commemorative patch on the left breast shows the team's success in Stanley Cup challenges. In 1908, the team celebrated being the holders of the title Champions of the World '06 '07 '08. Because of this patch, this sweater, more than 110 years old, was most likely worn during the 1908-09 Eastern Canada Amateur Hockey Association season. After Blachford retired, the Wanderers continued having success after turning professional in the National Hockey Association, as the team won the league's O'Brien Trophy and the Stanley Cup in 1910. The team also boasted several key Honoured Members like Ernie "Moose" Johnson, Lester Patrick, Art Ross and Ernie Russell. The Hall's artifact highlights the roots of professional hockey and the major impact that forgotten teams had on growing fan passion for the game.

Professional hockey did not exclusively exist on the East Coast. Rather, the Pacific Coast Hockey Association transformed the game by introducing the blue line and goal creases while allowing for more fluid game play with forward passing and goaltenders being allowed to drop to the ice to stop the puck. The Hall preserves two Seattle Metropolitans sweaters. The two artifacts belonged to Honoured Members Frank Foyston and Harry "Hap" Holmes, who helped guide the west-coast club to become the first team from the United States to win the Stanley Cup. The iconic red, green and white sweaters worn between 1915-24 provides an opportunity for visitors to consider how professional hockey expanded across national borders and the impact that this growth still has in the 21st century.

Though the NHA and the PCHA contributed to the growth of professional hockey, ultimately the National Hockey League reigned supreme. The Ottawa Senators dominated the league in the 1920s, successfully winning challenges for Lord Stanley's gift in 1920, 1921, twice in 1923, and in 1927. The Hall has regularly and proudly displayed Honoured Member Frank Nighbor's Senators sweater from 1923. Similar to the Seattle Metropolitans sweater, the Senators sweater boasts piercing red, white and black stripes (barber pole). Commemorating the team's Stanley Cup victory, a special patch across the chest denotes Ottawa as the 1922-23 World Champions. These four sweaters, spanning hockey's three early decades of competition and three different professional leagues, symbolize the reach of the sport across North America.

37

THE GREATEST COLLECTION

World Hockey Association supremacy was recognized with the Avco World Trophy *(below)*. WHA team colours and logos were certainly not uninteresting *(right)*.

A BITTER AND BOLD RIVAL

For five decades, the National Hockey League dominated as the premier professional league. In 1972, however, the World Hockey Association (WHA) emerged and enticed stars like Bobby Hull and Gordie Howe to join their ranks. Future Honoured Members like Mark Messier and Wayne Gretzky made their professional debuts in the WHA. This turbulent history resulted in a direct challenge to the Hall's effort to commemorate hockey's entire history, as the museum's sole financial patron at the time, the NHL initially did not want to celebrate its most formidable rival. Lefty Reid, the curator of the Hall, had to justify and secretly acquire these important pieces of history, even if this contradicted his role as an NHL employee. As a result of these early efforts, the Hall has been able to tell the complex history of professional hockey during the 1970s.

Reid justified his efforts to acquire Gordie Howe's WHA artifacts since the legend had already been enshrined as an Honoured Member and the pieces told the latest chapter of his contributions to hockey. Direct donations, meanwhile, also show the roots of the rival league. Terry Caffery donated his New England Whalers sweater from the team's and league's first season in 1972-73. That year, the team won the Avco World Trophy as WHA Champions and Caffery individually won the Lou Kaplan Trophy as the league's rookie of the year. It is part of the Hall's collection.

Today, the Hall continues to benefit from Lefty Reid's secret efforts to acquire WHA photos, media guides and game-worn artifacts.

Since the Hall today has more autonomy from the NHL than it did in the 1970s, these early curatorial efforts provide the basis for telling a more expansive history of the professional game. This greatly benefited the game of hockey and its history. As Reid himself has stated, and the Hall has built upon in the decades since his tenure as curator ended, his "pride and glory" during his time as curator are the efforts to build the Hall's library, which turned into the Resource Centre, as well as acquiring significant non-NHL artifacts like these WHA pieces. Since his tenure, the Hall has further emphasized Lefty's efforts by promoting the idea that hockey history extends beyond NHL accomplishments.

Current Curator Phil Pritchard views Lefty Reid's "vision" as being ahead of its time and the foundation on which current Hall leaders have built the museum's collection of WHA artifacts. He directly connects this radical collection-building approach to the revolutionary — and sometimes outlandish — characteristics of the rival league. As the "Keeper of the Cup" notes, "compared to the monotone jersey designs in the NHL, the WHA embraced the use of colour and unique designs." The Hall possesses examples of the league's infamous blue pucks, Garry Peters 1973-74 New York Golden Blades skates that have an all-white boot and a bold gold blade, and a bright yellow Cincinnati Stingers sweater. Because of the Hall's efforts to acquire artifacts that symbolize a direct challenge to traditional hockey evolution and achievement, fans are able to consider advances in the game's presentation and style and how these efforts reshaped the game that is enjoyed decades later.

CHAPTER 3 | GOING PRO

39

THE GREATEST COLLECTION

These are just some examples of the classic Howe and Gretzky artifacts in the Hall's collection.

GREATNESS AND HOWE!

No two players dominated hockey and captured imaginations quite like Gordie Howe and Wayne Gretzky. The icons set records, won championships and accepted the responsibility of role model, during their careers and following, with aplomb. And even though their playing time overlapped only briefly, the two are often spoken of in tandem, owing to a relationship borne of mutual respect — Gretzky idolized Howe as a boy near about the time Howe recognized Gretzky as a prodigy — and a friendship was nurtured over decades.

The two are also individually responsible for creating some of the greatest memories, and generating the most memorabilia, in hockey, much of the latter on permanent display at the Hall. Collectively, for a temporary display in 2019, they were celebrated on a single banner in *9 & 99: The Howe Gretzky Exhibition*, which featured artifacts from their careers, including the points at which they intersected. More than 150 items were featured in *9 & 99*, including the jacket Howe received as a signing bonus in 1946, Gretzky's first pair of skates and a famous, and playful, photo of the two together, one the wily veteran, the other the wide-eyed boy.

Beyond the content, the exhibition is just one example of how the Hall interprets and reimagines its own collection and continuously presents it to visitors in compelling ways.

CHAPTER 3 | GOING PRO

Humboldt strong.

HOCKEY WITH HEART

99.9 percent of the time, hockey, like many other sports, is a happy distraction to life. It offers joy, excitement, the occasional let-down and the opportunity to bond with likeminded supporters. It sometimes serves as an important vehicle for healing, both within its own ranks and also through outreach to the community.

The Vegas Golden Knights had yet to play a regular season NHL game in 2017 when a senseless shooting took the lives of 58 innocent people. Shortly after, at the inaugural home opener, the team rallied around a hurting city and nation to remember those who were lost and to pay tribute to first responders. Later that season, the Knights retired number 58, the elegant banner reverently stitched with the names of each of the victims.

Hockey similarly unites within its own ranks when tragedy strikes. The Humboldt Broncos bus crash in 2018 that took the lives of 16 members of the team led to an outpouring of support for the junior club and its Saskatchewan hometown that spanned virtually all hockey leagues all the way up to the NHL. In 1986, the Swift Current Broncos suffered the loss of four players in a bus crash while en route to a game. The players are remembered through the Four Broncos Memorial Trophy that's awarded annually to the Western Hockey League's player of the year. In 2011, a flight carrying the Lokomotiv Yaroslavl team of the Kontinental Hockey League crashed on take-off killing 44 people, including 26 players and three coaches. Tributes were immediate and widespread across the hockey world, especially in Russia, where an estimated 100,000 mourners attended a service at the team's home arena.

41

THE GREATEST COLLECTION

Jacques Plante put his stamp on hockey throughout his career, including lending his famous face to the fledgling Edmonton Oilers of the WHA to end it.

Skates from Plante's final year of pro hockey, 1974-75, are part of the Hall's collection. He entered the Hall three years later.

Wherever hockey is played, you will find Hockey Hall of Fame Curator Phil Pritchard (right) accepting a new artifact to add to the Hall's collection. In this case, he receives a jersey from Georgiy Kobylyanskiy of the KHL in 2019.

LATEST GREATEST

Today, a direct rival to the NHL does not exist, but the Russian-based Kontinental Hockey League represents a significant alternative for professional players. Founded in 2008, the league presently operates in six different nations. The Hall has made a conscious effort to collect and preserve KHL items, acquiring a number of artifacts from the 2018-19 playoff series, including: a playoff puck, a final play-off game puck, a Gagarin Cup gold medal and HC CSKA Moscow Captain Sergey Andronov's helmet, gloves and jersey from the final playoff-game when the team won the league championship. While the KHL has yet to match the WHA as a direct competitor to the NHL, the Hall continually reaches out to it and other leagues around the world to tell a more comprehensive narrative of hockey's history and connection to fans around the globe.

HONOURED TRAVELS

While the Hall's world view highlights the history of the game on a grand scale, the museum's holdings also allow for individual players to promote the sport's evolution. Gordie Howe, for example, began his career with the Detroit Red Wings in 1946 when the National Hockey League only had six teams. He retired after the 1970-71 season, achieving immediate enshrinement into the Hall in '72 since he held numerous prestigious NHL records.

The WHA coaxed him to come out of retirement in 1973 in order to play on the Houston Aeros with his sons Mark and Marty. After four seasons, he moved on to play for the New England Whalers and played in the WHA All-Star Game during the 1978-79 season with Wayne Gretzky. In 1979, the NHL absorbed four WHA teams including Gretzky's Edmonton Oilers, Bobby Hull's Winnipeg Jets and Réal Cloutier's Quebec Nordiques. Howe transitioned back to the NHL with the now-named Hartford Whalers and played his final season in 1979-80, which included an emotional homecoming during the 1980 NHL All-Star Game in Detroit. His multi-league and multi-decade career reflects the growth and evolution of professional hockey. As Mr. Hockey set scoring marks that stood for decades, the Hall's collection of his artifacts silently attests to these changes and accomplishments.

The WHA was pretty good at attracting star power to the league, including Frank Mahovlich as captain of the Toronto Toros.

THE GREATEST COLLECTION

A SABRE, A KNIGHT AND A COFFEE CUP?

Professional teams across the continent create and promote their own unique identity. Whether it is the Nashville Predators surprising fans with a different country star performing the U.S. National Anthem each playoff game or a Detroit Red Wings fan throwing an octopus onto the ice, tradition and symbolism define many teams. When the Buffalo Sabres entered the NHL in 1970, the team presented their inaugural season ticket holders with a 28-inch Wilkinson sword engraved with the team's logo and a facsimile signature of coach George "Punch" Imlach. The team instantly sought to differentiate themselves from other NHL teams and create a distinct identity with unique mementoes for their fans. The Hall recognizes this effort by preserving this stunning piece in their collection.

Most recently, the NHL has expanded to Las Vegas, where the Golden Knights' passion and very Vegas pageantry enthralled fans. The pre-game festivities and in-game energy during the team's drive to successfully reach the Stanley Cup Final during their inaugural season highlights the untapped potential for professional hockey. Beginning in the 2021-22 season, the National Hockey League will expand to 32 teams. The Seattle franchise will mark the next evolution for the NHL and the Hall will be prepared to preserve and commemorate this forthcoming chapter in hockey's development.

CHAPTER 3 | GOING PRO

Think it will set off the metal detector?! The Buffalo Sabres gifted two-foot-plus long sabres to season ticket holders in their first year in 1970. What an era!

FEATURED ARTIFACT

ONE LOOK AT GORDIE HOWE'S RED WINGS SKATES IS ALL IT TAKES TO APPRECIATE THAT ALL OF THE GOALS, RECORDS AND CHAMPIONSHIPS 'MR. HOCKEY' WRACKED UP BEFORE HANGING THEM UP IN 1971 WERE HARD FOUGHT AND EARNED. YET SOMEHOW THEY LOOK BOY-LIKE, ALMOST HUMBLE, CERTAINLY WHEN COMPARED WITH MODERN-DAY EQUIPMENT.

BUT ALL THE TECHNOLOGY AND SCIENCE IN THE WORLD CAN'T REPLACE THE TRUE EMOTION OF THE ARTIFACT, INCLUDING THE BATTLE-MARKED BOOTS, TAPED TOE CAPS, PLASTIC END CAPS AND THE WELL-GROUND BLADES. THE NO. 9 ON THE SIDES IS PURE ELEGANCE.

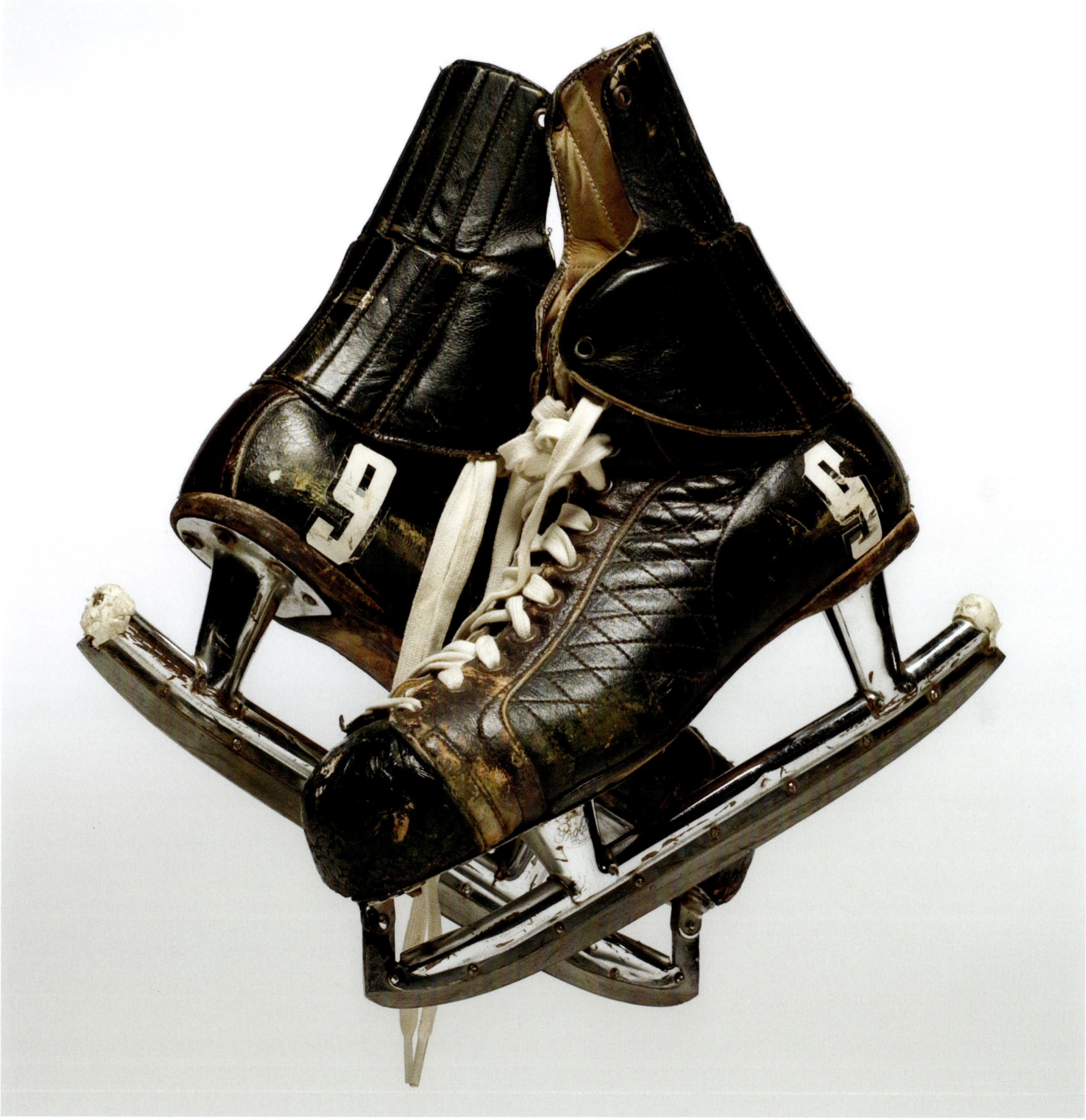

THE GREATEST COLLECTION

CHAPTER 4
TRAILBLAZERS AND WARRIORS
Honouring Game-Changers

The Hockey Hall of Fame's mission is to celebrate hockey as a uniting force. While the museum provides a complex narrative of the game's participation by focusing on multiple professional and amateur leagues, the institution also celebrates how hockey has broken through gender, racial, cultural and even national barriers. Military honour and outreach, Indigenous participation and disabled accessibility have also allowed numerous people to enjoy the sport and share its values, including its ability to heal.

HONOURING SERVICE

Hockey and military service have been connected since World War I. With the creation of the Memorial Cup and the Hall's enshrinement of war heroes like U.S. amateur star Hobey Baker, the collection honours the sacrifice that many players and communities have made to their nation. Each Remembrance Day in Canada, Veterans' Day in the United States, the Hall places red ribbons on the plaques of Honoured Members of the inductees who served their nations. Players like Milt Schmidt, Bobby Bauer, Woody Dumart and Johnny Bower all receive recognition for service to country in addition to their significant hockey achievements. Additionally, the Hall partnered with Library and Archives Canada to create a special educational program for visiting school groups to better understand the sacrifices soldiers have made across generations.

The museum possesses medals awarded to Conn Smythe, the dynamic force behind the Toronto Maple Leafs for decades, from his service in both the First and Second World Wars. More recently, the Hall unveiled a special exhibit for Canada's 150th anniversary that allowed visitors to take a photo with a section of the Kandahar Rink Boards, part of the beloved ball hockey rink set up at the Canadian

Hobey Baker was a leader on the ice and in the service of his country. The inaugural member of the Hall was a commander of U.S. 141st Aero Squadron in World War I.

Forces Airbase in Afghanistan from 2006 to 2011. The unique artifact shows the tremendous wear from use by the men and women serving to protect freedom, and allows visitors to reflect on both the sacrifices service requires and the recreational opportunities — in this case, something uniquely Canadian — that helps relieve the stress of duty. Notable game participants, beyond the soldiers themselves, have included Hall inductees like (Chairman) Lanny McDonald who, while visiting with the troops, joined in a game that was halted by a dust storm. It reminded players of outdoor rink games back in Canada that were interrupted by snowstorms.

The Hall's collection also celebrates the therapeutic and restorative aspects of hockey. A jersey from the Ohio Warriors, a sledge hockey affiliate of the USA Warriors Ice Hockey Program for disabled war veterans, shows how the sport can be enjoyed by all and is a reminder of the strong will and desire to participate in the game.

Rink boards from the Canadian Forces Airbase in Afghanistan show the wear and tear of service to the military.

Members of the Canadian military's 25th Brigade battle it out on the Imjin River in Korea in 1953. The Imjin Hockey Classic is now an annual re-enactment of the historic game played to honour Korean War veterans.

THE GREATEST COLLECTION

A CULTURAL REVOLUTION

While there can be no greater achievement for a hockey player than to be inducted into the Hall, a select few are bestowed the status of pioneer for their athletic achievements as well as their role in growing the sport within their community. Beverly "Bev" Beaver was a pioneer. Not only did she star in women's hockey, she also was a standout softball player and a decorated bowler. She became a role model for Indigenous players for her athletic achievements and for overcoming racism and sexism throughout her multi-sport career. Although she could only participate in male exhibition contests as a teenager, the Mohawk from Southern Ontario's Six Nations Reserve later played in women's tournaments and won the prestigious Regional Tom Longboat Award in 1967 as well as the national level of the award in 1980. The award dates to 1951 and recognizes aboriginal athletes for their outstanding contributions to sport in Canada. The Hall proudly preserves her Burlington Ladies Hockey Team sweater, patches from various tournaments in which she played as well as one of her MVP trophies — she won five!

The museum also acquired a significant early twentieth century stick in order to tell the story of how hockey can both be strengthened by diversity and assist society in becoming more inclusive. It belonged to Charles "Charlie" Lightfoot, one of the first black players in organized hockey and who was the descendant of a Kentucky slave. Lightfoot played for the Stratford Hockey Club from 1900-05 and won the OHA Junior Championship. The artifact relates the inclusive potential of hockey dating back to the very origins of the sport.

The Hall's collection includes Danielle Goyette's Team Quebec jersey from the 1996 Esso Cup Women's National Championship. Goyette, named tournament Top Forward, scored all three goals in the final to lead her team to the Abby Hoffman Cup win.

CHAPTER 4 | TRAILBLAZERS AND WARRIORS

Larry Kwong was a member of the Alexander Cup-winning Valleyfield Braves in the 1950-51 season, and an early face of diversity in hockey.

BEV BEAVER "1983" BURLINGTON LADIES HOCKEY TEAM

Bev Beaver was an icon in her Mohawk community as a standout in three sports and as a role model for Indigenous women.

Charlie Lightfoot was a descendant of a slave, hockey champion and one of the earliest pioneers for diversity in hockey. His 100-year-old stick is a valuable part of the Hall's collection.

51

THE GREATEST COLLECTION

This sled was made by Lou Mulvihill during the early years of sledge hockey. Mulvihill won a bronze medal with Team Canada at the 1994 Winter Paralympics.

From sledge to electric wheelchair, athletes everywhere prove that hockey is accessible to everyone.

52

CHAPTER 4 | TRAILBLAZERS AND WARRIORS

The artifacts from these two pioneers form a key part of the Hall's initiative titled *The Changing Face of Hockey – Diversity in Our Game*. The program seeks to "pay homage to the pioneers who confronted discrimination from the hockey world through their perseverance, talent and courage. They have enriched the cultural landscape of hockey and established a tangible forum in which to fight prejudices still faced by many, both in hockey and in life." The institution's educational program provides study material for students to prepare for their visit as well as answer questions while evaluating the exhibit. As a result, the Hall shares the rich history and complexity of hockey and allows all visitors to consider how they can apply the lessons learned from the sport to their daily interactions. The Hall's message that hockey transcends any physical, cultural or social distinctions creates the most significant foundation of the museum's narrative to visitors.

(Left to right) Ossie Carnegie, Herb Carnegie and Manny McIntyre were linemates with the Sherbrooke Randies of the Quebec Provincial Hockey League during the 1945-46 season.

Jordin Tootoo was all about firsts: He was the first Inuk player and the first player to grow up in Nunavut to participate in the NHL.

53

THE GREATEST COLLECTION

Hall artifacts to honour military service include an RCAF squadron sweater, a team photo of the first winners of the Memorial Cup (WWI) and Conn Smythe's medals (WWI and II).

"FROM FAILING HANDS…"

"Hockey does it like no one else when it comes to honouring the veterans and those who sacrificed the ultimate," Phil Pritchard, curator at the Hall, once said.

You can certainly include the Hockey Hall of Fame in any conversation about recognizing the men and women who have served their countries in wartime. Whether poignant gestures like placing red ribbons each Remembrance Day on the plaques of Honoured Members in the Great Hall who served in the military, or presenting full exhibitions like *Hockey Marching as to War: The First World War and a Century of Military Ties to the Game*, the museum pays tribute to veterans and active personnel.

Beyond the displays, the Hall holds in its collection several major artifacts that commemorate fallen heroes. These include the Memorial Cup, awarded to the national junior champions each year, that honours the Canadian service men and women lost in the First World War, the Joseph Turner Memorial Cup, previously awarded to the International Hockey League champs and named for the American Hockey League goalie who was killed in 1944 fighting in the Second World War as a member of the U.S. Army, and a Military Cross that was awarded to legendary Maple Leafs owner Conn Smythe for his heroism in the First World War as a member of the Canadian Artillery. He had enlisted in the military a week after winning the Ontario Hockey Association junior championship in 1915.

Beyond the Hall, the NHL community shows ongoing respect to veterans in numerous and touching ways, both on team and individual levels. The Anaheim Ducks, for example, present a glass plaque to a soldier at each home game to honour their service, while the Toronto Maple Leafs have hosted reunions where families are surprised by a loved one in active duty returning home. Kyle Palmieiri of the New Jersey Devils began a program that donated tickets to military families, and the Florida Panthers once surprised a wounded veteran with a mortgage-free home.

Indeed, hockey does it like no one else.

CHAPTER 4 | TRAILBLAZERS AND WARRIORS

Hockey historian Kevin Shea *(left)* and Hockey Hall of Fame Vice-President and Curator Phil Pritchard, engage Indigenous students through selected artifacts and stories. Students Marcus Allen and Kerrigan MacLean, both from Mine Centre Public School in Mine Centre, ON, visit their designs on display at the Hall.

NORTHERN EXPOSURE

In 2019, the Hall partnered with Connected North, a network service provider that delivers immersive and interactive education platforms to Indigenous schools in remote northern communities through high-definition two-way video communication and collaboration technology. The system connects students with experts, content partners and educational venues like museums to enhance curriculum and add exciting new resources to the classroom. Commitment to Indigenous perspectives and reconciliation lies at the heart of the program, including developing culturally relevant material and introducing First Nations, Métis and Inuit role models wherever possible.

The goal of the outreach is to provide Indigenous schools with access to engaging and empowering hockey-related content. Through the support of the The Larry and Judy Tanenbaum Family Legends of Hockey Scholars Fund, the Hall developed and delivered two hour-long, live virtual field trip curriculums, namely "The Power of Team" and "Leaders & Groundbreakers" that examine the composition of a group, or more specifically, successful hockey teams, and leadership skills and development. Both curriculums include video tours of Hall exhibits, interactive class activities, as well as artifacts, historical footage and archival photographs.

The sessions gave participating students the opportunity to complete a post-session assignment challenge and to be recognized as a Legends of Hockey Scholar including an all-expense paid trip to experience the Hockey Hall of Fame in Toronto, as well as a financial contribution towards their future education.

A GAME FOR ALL

The Hall's Selection Committee has continually expanded the museum's membership to reflect the changing face of hockey. In 2018, Willie O'Ree led that year's class, which celebrated unity, diversity and inclusion. An earlier significant inclusion, however, began in 2010 when the by-laws changed to permit the enshrinement of female players as Honoured Members. The first inductees included Canadian Angela James and American Cammi Granato. Through 2019, seven women have added a critical and necessary dimension to the Hall's celebration of hockey's history and evolution.

In addition to these formal members, the Hall's collection showcases significant contributions of women to the sport. Shannon Szabados succeeded while competing against both women and men. The goaltender backstopped the Canadian women's national team to a gold medal in both the 2010 and 2014 Winter Olympic Games. The Hall also preserves artifacts that highlight her club team accomplishments that include being named the first-ever female goaltender to be named the first star of the game after recording a 33-shot shutout for the Columbus Cottonmouths of the Southern Professional Hockey League on December 26, 2015. The jersey, blocker and stick she used in the game are now part of the Hall's collection, standing as reminders to fans and visitors of the impressive advancement of women's hockey.

The Hall's collection extends past on-ice accomplishments and achievements and also speaks to changes, transitions, and unity in society and communities. As new milestones and voices emerge and shape hockey history, the Hall will continue to include contributions that often transcend the sport itself.

GREAT CONNECTION

Hockey has also inspired international diplomacy and conjured a friendly rivalry between U.S. and Canadian leaders. Alongside innumerable more traditional hockey artifacts in the Hall's collection sit two cases of beer. When the two nations competed for the gold medal at the 2010 Winter Olympics in Vancouver, President Barack Obama and Prime Minister Stephen Harper made a friendly wager. Each leader chose a brewery significant to their nation: D.G. Yuengling & Son and Molson, each of which is the oldest brewery in their respective nation. The Hall's collection and showcase of these unique items, therefore, highlights how passion for sport united two neighbouring nations as they watched athletes compete on the highest international platform.

The Hall's collection includes items of high politics and diplomacy: two cases of beer. The suds were negotiated prior to the Canada-U.S. Gold Medal game in 2010, between national leaders Stephen Harper and Barack Obama, amounting to a friendly lager...er, wager.

CHAPTER 4 | TRAILBLAZERS AND WARRIORS

Too many men on the ice! Shannon Szabados' accomplishments as a goalie, including her two Olympic golds and her shutout performance in a professional men's league, are on proud display at the Hall.

57

FEATURED ARTIFACT

L'HONORABLE MAURICE RICHARD, P.C., C.C., O.Q.

A HERO IN THE WORLD OF SPORTS, HE CAN STILL ELECTRIFY CROWDS BY HIS MERE PRESENCE. IN THE EARLY 1980s HE BECAME A SPECIAL AMBASSADOR FOR THE MONTREAL CANADIENS HOCKEY CLUB.

THIS PROUD, COURAGEOUS MAN IS TYPICAL OF HIS GENERATION OF PLAYERS FOR WHOM IT WAS IMPORTANT THAT HOCKEY BE PLAYED FOR HONOUR AND FOR THE JOY OF THE FANS. HIS NAME IS KNOWN THE WORLD OVER, AND THIRTY-EIGHT YEARS AFTER HIS RETIREMENT HE REMAINS ONE OF HOCKEY'S MOST POPULAR FIGURES. THIS IS A PROMOTION WITHIN THE ORDER.

- THE GOVERNOR GENERAL OF CANADA (RICHARD'S ORDER OF CANADA)

59

THE GREATEST COLLECTION

CHAPTER 5
PERSONAL TREASURES
A History of Hockey Told Through Trading Cards

Of all the big and shiny objects at the Hockey Hall of Fame — and there are lots — it's a bit curious to think that among the most popular artifacts on display are 2.5-inch-by-3.5-inch pieces of cardboard with grainy photos and a distinct bubblegum smell. Such is their simple yet alluring ability to draw fans to a favourite player, and power to take us back to a time and place when virtually everyone traded in the game's most popular artifacts.

CARDBOARD CONNECTION

In addition to the equipment, trophies and interactive features at the Hall, the preservation of thousands upon thousands of hockey cards, including those on display, provide a relatable opportunity for visitors while also telling the history of hockey through printed images. As the Hall of Fame's collection shows, for more than a century many of the sport's greatest icons have had their stories told through these cards, giving fans the opportunity to possess artifacts that connect them with hockey's most memorable ambassadors.

Three of the earliest hockey card sets produced were distributed in cigarette packs. The 1910 C56, 1911 C55 and 1912 C57 sets showcase stars from teams across Canada. These three sets show both the expansion and the durability of hockey during this early era of the professional game. For example, Honoured Member Tom Dunderdale's three cards illustrate the trajectory of his career. His C56 card depicts him as a member of the Montreal Shamrocks, the C55 card shows him with the Quebec Bulldogs and the C57 card — while still picturing him in a Quebec sweater — notes that the player had moved across the country by showing that he now played for the Victoria Senators of the Pacific Coast Hockey Association.

A portrait of Tommy Dunderdale shows the early star as a member of the Victoria Aristocrats of the Pacific Coast Hockey Association. Dunderdale was inducted into the Hockey Hall of Fame in 1974.

Dunderdale's turn-of-the-20th-century hockey card is a valuable part of the Hall's collection.

THE GREATEST COLLECTION

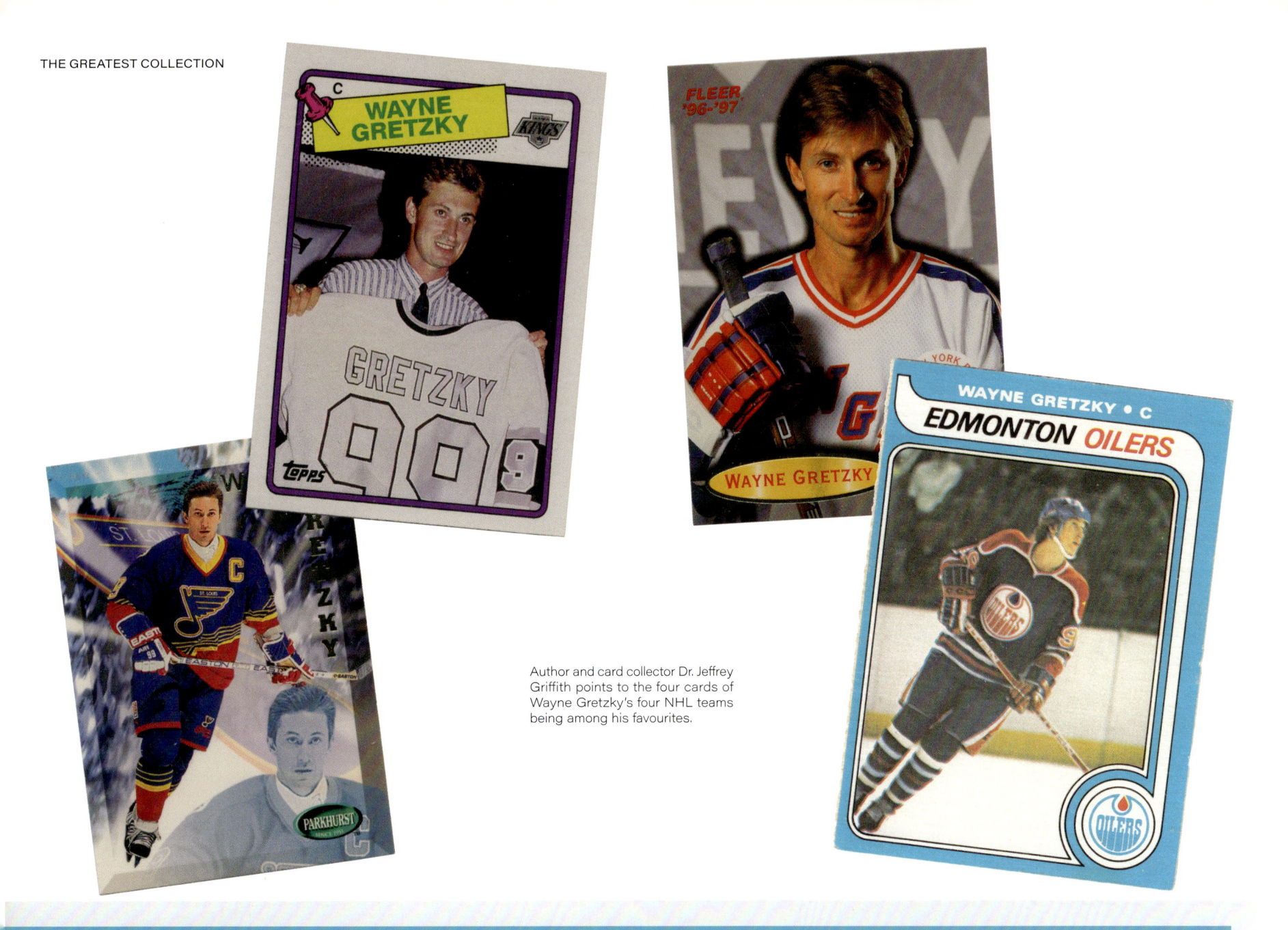

Author and card collector Dr. Jeffrey Griffith points to the four cards of Wayne Gretzky's four NHL teams being among his favourites.

IN PURSUIT OF GREATNESS

How much impact can a single artifact have on a person's life? Well, in the case of Dr. Jeffrey Griffith, author, historian and owner of one of the greatest private hockey card collections, plenty.

It all began when Griffith was nine years old and was given a puck signed by Wayne Gretzky while attending a game between the Mighty Ducks of Anaheim and the Los Angeles Kings. Griffith would come to idolize Gretzky, and begin collecting cards and sets related to the Great One's career. A decade later, he had amassed one of the largest and most complete Gretzky card collections in the world.

Griffith has become an authority in the card-trading community, attending all major events in Canada and the U.S., and is regularly featured in newspapers and magazines because of his knowledge. He is also passionate about the Hockey Hall of Fame and its collection, and is known around the Hall's Resource Centre where he spent a considerable amount of time while researching his master's thesis on hockey and its impact on Canadian culture.

Over the past several years, Griffith has been assembling an award-winning Hockey Hall of Fame collection. Rookie and first cards from virtually every Honoured Member form the backbone of the collection, while Significant Singles show the trajectory of players' legendary careers. Game-used memorabilia cards showcase embedded artifacts that icons used during their playing days that help create lasting moments for fans to recall.

Griffith's collection also includes autographs — whether on cards, documents or acquired in person — an important way in which fans have interacted with the game's greats over time. Taken together, the diverse collection highlights the growth of hockey and how the shrine has commemorated the game since the first induction class of 1945.

- Editor

CHAPTER 5 | PERSONAL TREASURES

It's hard to imagine buying anything for pennies these days, but there was a time when a few cents could land some real hockey treasures — and a stick of gum.

TRADING NAMES

Trading cards have carried unique names and descriptions throughout the years. In more modern times, cataloguers have attached identifying labels to some of hockey's earliest sets. For example, sets produced by various tobacco or chocolate companies have been assigned more consistent labels such as C55 and V145. Over time, however, iconic brand names have resonated with collectors.

O-Pee-Chee, Parkhurst and Upper Deck are just a few of the names that have become synonymous with quality and historical significance. Indeed, as a new product under each banner is released, the new set adds to the legacy of hockey history.

Enjoyed alongside the more traditional artifacts that the Hall has collected over the previous decades, hockey cards provide fans with the opportunity to follow players' evolution from rookies into sporting icons.

Trading cards have dramatically evolved from simple pieces of cardboard with images printed on the front stored in either cigarette or wax packs. Upper Deck introduced and has revolutionized the industry with high-gloss cards safely inserted into foil packs. Further, virtually every NHL licensed set now includes some combination of game-used memorabilia cards and autograph cards from past, present and future stars of the game.

Third-party authenticators have also created a grading system that seeks to ensure the authentication and preservation of cards spanning over a century of hockey history. Professional Sports Authenticators (PSA), for example, rates cards on a scale of 1 to 10, with 10 being gem mint condition. As hockey history and the trading card industry continue to develop, fans have a unique and evolving way to connect to the game's ever-changing landscape.

THE GREATEST COLLECTION

Jack Laviolette of the Montreal Nationals is shown in this portrait from the 1903-04 season. His hockey card, meanwhile, has him in the sweater of the Canadian Club.

Cards in the Hall's collection can also visually depict a team's evolution. For example, the Montreal Canadiens have existed for more than a century, and though their current jersey is now iconic, the team proudly wore a number of different colours and logos throughout their existence. On Jack Laviolette's 1910 C56 card, for example, the Canadiens have a shocking blue sweater with a white C emblazoned on front. On Newsy Lalonde's C55 rookie card, the team wore a more familiar red sweater but had a green patched logo. Though the card is in black and white, Aurèle Joliat's 1923 rookie card from V145-1 William Paterson shows the now iconic Montreal jersey and logo. A 1924 Champ's Cigarette card of Georges Vézina pictures the goaltending legend wearing a commemorative logo celebrating the Canadiens' Stanley Cup victory in the 1923-24 season.

From the 1930s onward, cards have illustrated the dominance and greatness of the team's players and championship clubs all wearing the now familiar colour scheme and logo. Key rookie cards show the evolution of the club and its uniforms through the legendary players. Be it Toe Blake in 1937, Rocket Richard in 1951, Jacques Plante in 1955, Ken Dryden and Guy Lafleur in 1971, Patrick Roy in 1986 or Carey Price in 2007, these important cards allow fans to access, collect and treasure cardboard artifacts of past and present generations of players.

CHAPTER 5 | PERSONAL TREASURES

Aurèle Joliat's Montreal Canadiens player card, misspelled first name notwithstanding, is a prized part of the Hall's collection, as is his signature black peaked cap.

65

THE GREATEST COLLECTION

THE EVOLUTION OF

c.1870

1910

Hockey cards are tiny time capsules. Each provides a glimpse of an era, whether hair style, sweater style or image style (posed or action), lending a sense of time and place as much as insight into a player's career. Over the years, and we're talking centuries, the cards depict the game from its very origin to the modern day through imagery that ranges from early illustrations to simple black and white photography (some older cards had no information on the back at all) and to high-gloss action shots. And while technology, especially relating to photography and printing, continues to drive their evolution, much of the fascination surrounding cards relates to the past. Such is the nature of time capsules.

The following timeline features hockey cards from the Hockey Hall of Fame's collection, and skates readers through 14 decades of memories.

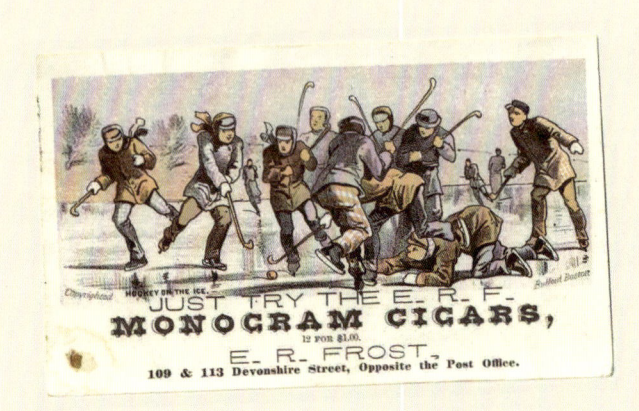

March 3, 1875 Two teams of nine players face off at Montreal's Victoria rink in what is widely considered the first official game of hockey.

Early sets celebrated the birth of professional hockey. The Newsy Lalonde card was famously printed with two different numbers.

1930

Dec. 16, 1929 The NHL adopts the offside rule.

Pre-War cards are sets that were produced before the start of World War II. The Hall's collection from this era celebrates hockey across North America. Not only do these cards illustrate the growth of professional hockey, but amateur players were also immortalized. O-Pee-Chee continues to contribute to hockey card history since its introduction in 1933.

66

CHAPTER 5 | PERSONAL TREASURES

HOCKEY CARDS

1920

Nov. 22-26, 1917 The National Hockey League is founded in Montreal.

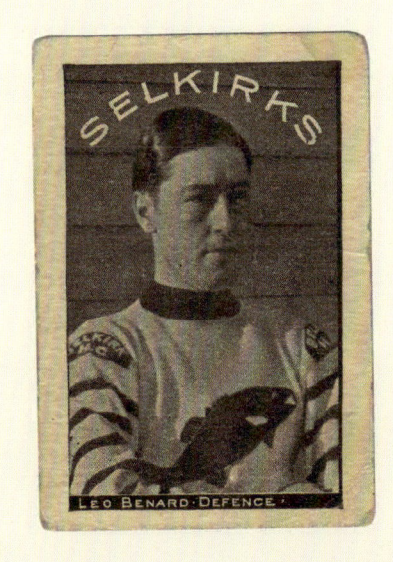

Beehive cards from the mid-1930s through the 1940s provided fans an opportunity to collect images of their favourite players. Both Parkhurst and Topps produced key rookie cards of National Hockey League legends over the next two decades. Parkhurst woud release the first mainstream set in the 1950s, giving birth to the modern hockey card era.

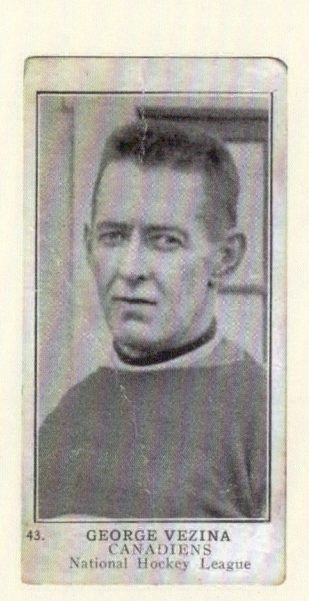

March 22, 1923 A hockey game is broadcast over the radio for the first time. Honoured Member Foster Hewitt handles the play-by-play.

67

THE GREATEST COLLECTION

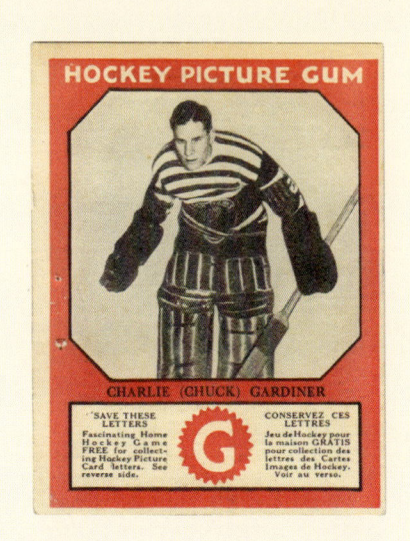

Nov. 12, 1931 Maple Leaf Gardens opens in Toronto.

1950

Nov. 1, 1952 Hockey Night in Canada debuts on television with a broadcast from Toronto's Maple Leaf Gardens.

CHAPTER 5 | PERSONAL TREASURES

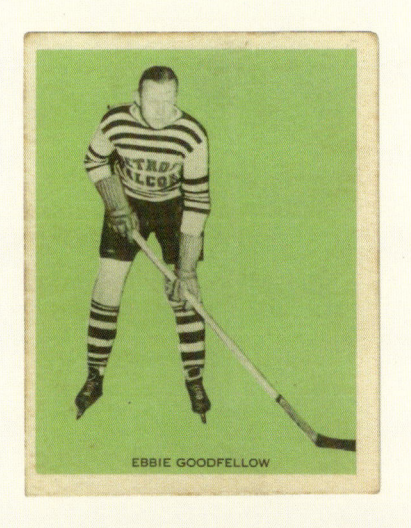

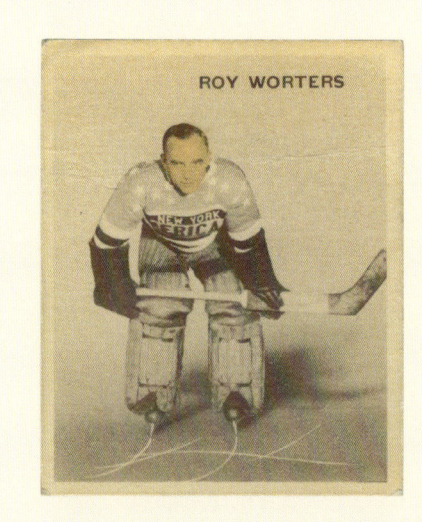

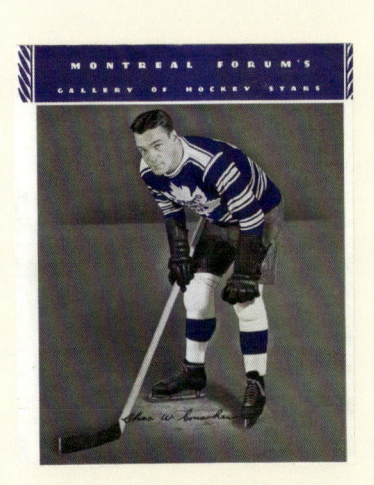

Nov 10, 1934 The first NHL penalty shot goal is scored by Ralph Bowman of the St. Louis Eagles in the team's only year of existence.

1940

1937 Captain James Sutherland of Kingston, ON, begins lobbying for the creation of a Hockey Hall of Fame after the Baseball Hall of Fame is founded a year earlier.

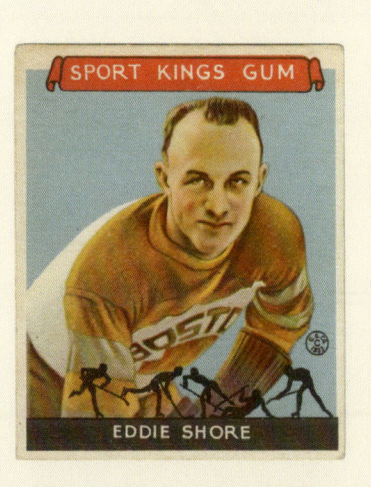

Oct. 13, 1947 The first NHL All-Star Game is played.

69

THE GREATEST COLLECTION

1960

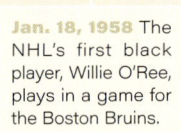

Jan. 18, 1958 The NHL's first black player, Willie O'Ree, plays in a game for the Boston Bruins.

Aug. 26, 1961 The first permanent Hockey Hall of Fame opens inside the Canadian Sports Hall of Fame. More than 750,000 people visit it that first year.

1980

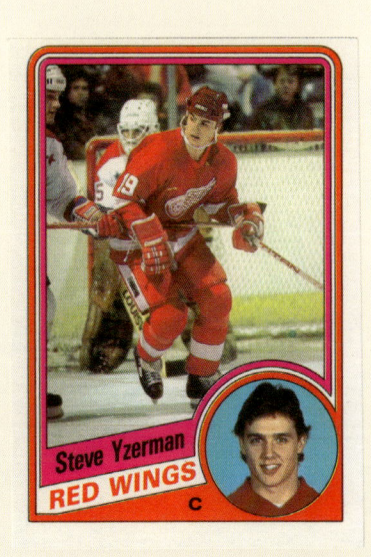

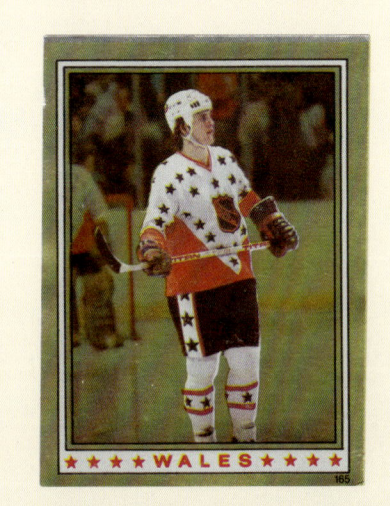

May 27, 1982 The Colorado Rockies move to New Jersey where they become the Devils.

June 22, 1979 Four teams from the defunct WHA, Edmonton, Winnipeg, Quebec and Hartford, join the NHL.

CHAPTER 5 | PERSONAL TREASURES

Feb. 9, 1966 The six-team NHL announces plans to add six more for the 1967-68 season. The Original Six era is over.

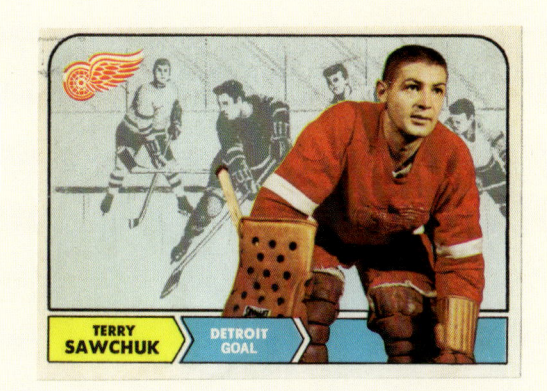

Cards from the late 1960s and throughout the 1970s reflect the growth and rivalry of professional hockey. O-Pee-Chee, Topps, Parkhurst and various local card sets celebrated the NHL's expansion, while the rival WHA had card sets dedicated to its vibrant team colours. Cards from the 1980s showcase a stabilization of professional hockey and promote dozens of iconic rookie cards as well as future Hall Honoured Members.

1970

Oct. 11, 1972 The 12-team World Hockey Association begins play in Ottawa.

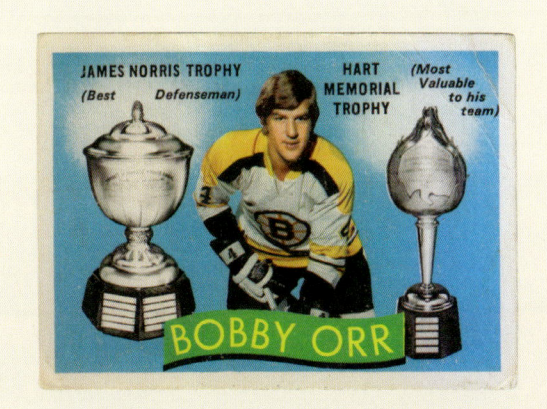

71

THE GREATEST COLLECTION

1990

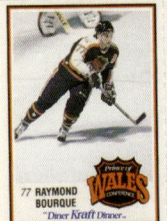

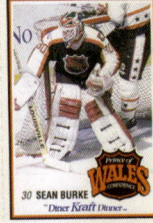

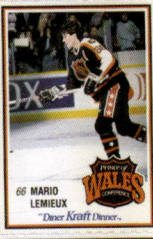

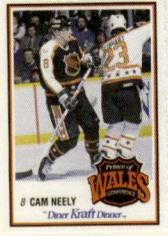

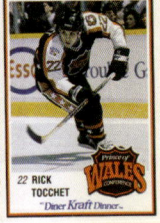

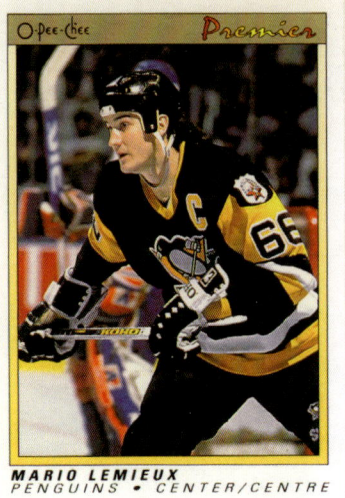

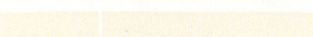

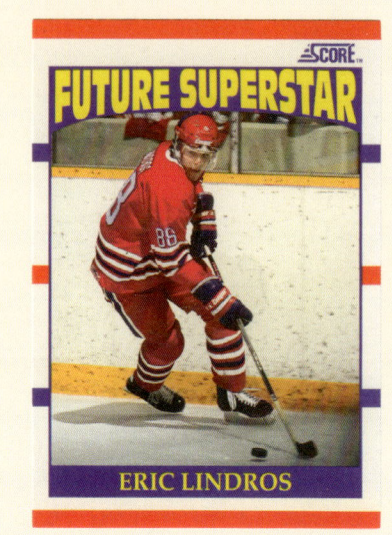

March 19-25, 1990 In Ottawa, the first World Women's Championship is held. Canada wins.

2000

The 2000s and 2010s boast many rookie cards of the NHL's present superstars and burgeoning legends. Each set builds upon the legacy of cards from the previous century. The passion to collect and trade these treasures continues to drive fans of all ages to these remarkable artifacts that play an important role in the telling of hockey and history.

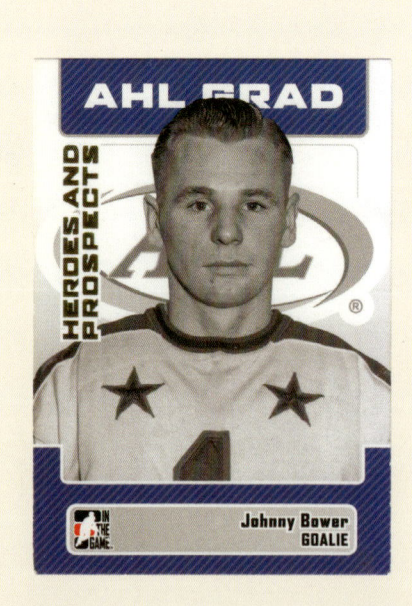

Nov. 8, 2010 Canadian Angela James and the U.S.'s Cammi Granato become the first women players inducted into the Hockey Hall of Fame.

72

CHAPTER 5 | PERSONAL TREASURES

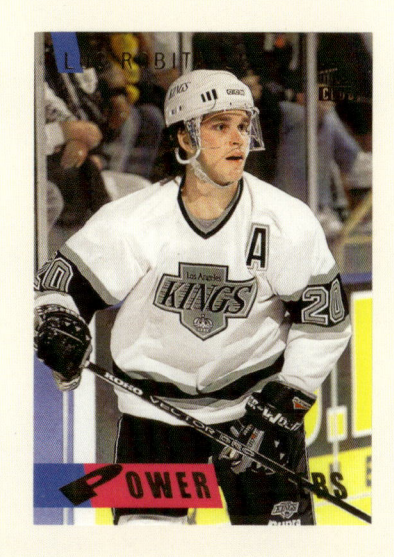

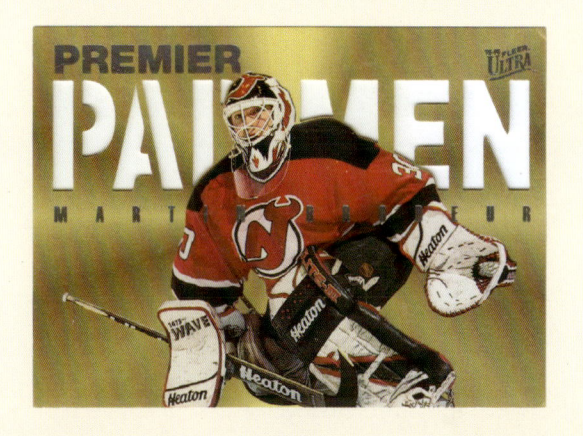

June 18, 1993 The Hockey Hall of Fame opens to the public in its new location, a former Bank of Montreal building on Front St. in downtown Toronto.

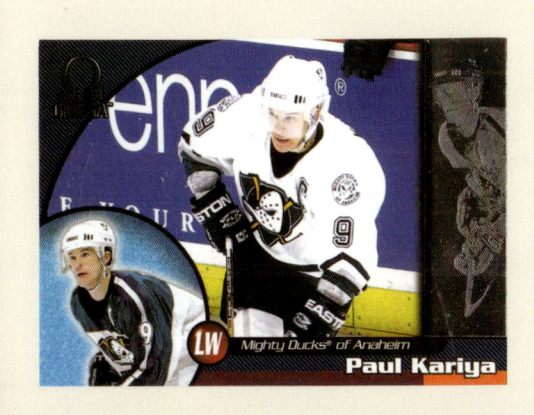

The 1990s saw a revolution in hockey cards. Companies like Upper Deck pushed cards from simple cardboard to glossy pieces of art and distributed them in sleek foil packs rather than clunky wax holders. Further, the introduction of insert sets, autograph cards and game-used memorabilia cards dramatically increased fan and collector interest.

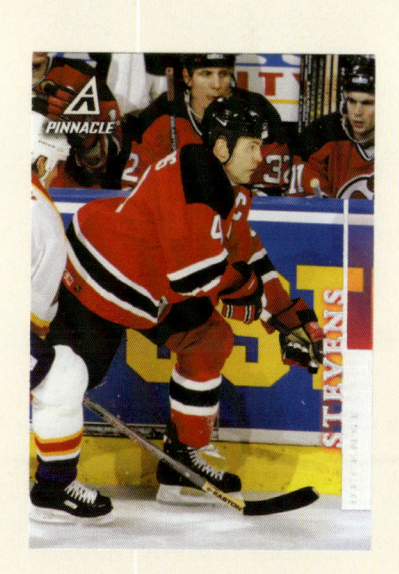

Oct. 3-4, 1997 The Mighty Ducks of Anaheim and Vancouver Canucks open the 1997-98 season in Tokyo, Japan, the first official NHL games played outside of North America.

73

THE GREATEST COLLECTION

CHOCOLATE AND BUBBLE GUM

The Hall's collection also hints at an additional appeal cards have held beyond connecting to hockey history. While acquiring cards and stats on a person's favourite player has always been important, occasionally the lure of an additional prize has further helped sell the product. The 1923 V128 Paulin's set — which showcased teams from the Western Canada Hockey League and boasts key rookie cards of Honoured Members Red Dutton, Bill Cook and George Hainsworth — informed collectors that they could send in "a complete set of seventy Famous Hockey Players' Pictures" for either a hockey stick or a box of chocolates. This brand synergy used cards to connect Paulin's products with an audience of hockey fans.

The most common hockey card promotion over the years was the inclusion of bubble gum in each pack. Included in products for decades through the 1980s, the gum often dried out, disintegrated or could even fuse to the card closest to the sugary substance. For generations of fans, the combination of sports and candy evokes vivid memories of childhood collecting and trading cards with friends while also learning about the accomplishments of their favourite sports heroes. This personal connection that people make when obtaining these pieces of hockey lore makes cards a consequential and important purveyor of hockey history.

...the combination of sports and candy evokes vivid memories of childhood collecting and trading cards with friends...

Albert Pudas was the first player born in Finland to play in the NHL.

CHAPTER 5 | PERSONAL TREASURES

CARD EVOLUTION

Rather than relying on stale bubble gum to promote its products, Upper Deck introduced numerous additional ways in which fans could get closer to the game. Autograph cards, game-used memorabilia cards and appearances at conventions all seek to connect the game with fans and collectors and contribute to the telling of the history and evolution of the sport. The Hall has been able to showcase and preserve some of the most iconic cards featuring "Young Guns," veterans and, of course, the game's greatest legends. Alongside other artifacts celebrating players' accomplishments, the Hall also possesses important cards of current hockey superstars like Sidney Crosby, Alexander Ovechkin and Connor McDavid.

As players today and in the future create lasting hockey memories, cards will continue to serve as an accessible means for fans of all ages to celebrate and interact with their personal heroes. As a result, the Hall's vast card collection will continue to grow and add to the rich storytelling of hockey — 2.5 by 3.5 inches at a time.

GREAT CONNECTION

Cards allow fans to interact, learn and collect information about the game's past, and to also follow the careers of contemporary players. Whether cards are carefully stored in binders and toploaders — special plastic cases that protect them from damage — or kept in shoe boxes and forgotten in a basement or attic, each one tells a unique story about the game and a fan's association with the sport. Since 1990, Upper Deck has carried the mantle of producing cutting-edge hockey trading cards. Upon their arrival and the acquisition of Wayne Gretzky as their spokesman, the California-based company introduced high-gloss cards in foil packs, a dramatic improvement over the rough cardboard available in wax packs. Additionally, the company has sponsored a popular exhibit at the Hall called *Upper Deck Collectors' Corner*.

Nikita Kucherov is the latest in a long list of NHL stars from Russia.

FEATURED ARTIFACT

EVERY ITEM IN THE HALL RELATES BACK TO THE PURSUIT OF THE NOT-ALWAYS ROUND AND NOT-ALWAYS RUBBER BLACK OBJECT THAT GRABS EVERYONE'S ATTENTION THE MOMENT IT'S DROPPED ON THE ICE.

THE PUCK BEGAN LIFE AS A WOODEN SQUARE IN THE LATE 1800s AS A REPLACEMENT FOR A BALL, WHICH HAD A HARD TIME STAYING IN PLAY. WOOD GAVE WAY TO RUBBER WITH THE SLICING OF THE CURVES.

MONTREAL'S VICTORIA HOCKEY CLUB INTRODUCED THE FIRST ROUND PUCKS IN THE 1880s. THE MODERN PUCK IS ONE INCH THICK, THREE INCHES IN DIAMETER AND WEIGHS 5.5-6 OUNCES. THEY'RE FROZEN BEFORE GAMES TO REDUCE BOUNCING — DNA BEING WHAT IT IS.

APPROVED
NHL
MADE IN CANADA
VICEROY MFG. CO. LTD.
NATIONAL HOCKEY LEAGUE
NHL
MADE IN CANADA ©NHL

THE GREATEST COLLECTION

CHAPTER 6
'THE GOAL WAS ASSISTED BY...'
The Hall's Outreach

Hockey's influence extends much farther and wider than the bright lights and big arenas of professional leagues. Likewise, the Hockey Hall of Fame's reach extends far beyond its museum in downtown Toronto. The Hall actively connects with communities far and wide to share the stories and values of the game, but also to learn and collect experiences and artifacts to add to its collection. This symbiotic relationship lies at the heart of the Hall's Outreach Program, and helps to ensure that grassroots content always has an equal place alongside the museum's famous trophies and awards.

This pass got Bobby Hewitson onto the CNE grounds in 1964 and into his own Hockey Hall of Fame. It was positively not transferable.

ROAD TRIP

The Hall has consistently worked to bring people into its exhibition space as well as reaching out to those who are unable to visit in person. Bobby Hewitson first developed tours of the Hall's exhibits at the Canadian National Exhibition in the 1960s in an effort to reach out to the local community. School field trips, scout troops, tourists and visiting fans all represented potential groups that could visit the CNE during non-exhibition times. Today, the Hall promotes the benefits and educational opportunities that its exhibitions offer. As their promotion for school groups states, "let the passion of hockey ignite the passion for learning! The Hockey Hall of Fame is an excellent educational and entertaining destination for your school field trip." Since the opening of the building at the CNE, the Hall has sought to be a magnet to the surrounding community to explore and interact with hockey history.

Over time the institution has been able to dedicate parts of its collection for travel around the globe. As Manager of Outreach Exhibits Izak Westgate shares, these events allow the Hall to reach fans who may not otherwise be able to travel to Toronto. The program tailors exhibits to the specific audience and brings artifacts of legendary and current stars to fans of all ages. Additionally, interactive games and trophies further connect the sport to a community. Moreover, travelling exhibits allow the museum to make new contacts with hockey communities in an effort to add to the Greatest Collection and hear how hockey has affected a specific location or group.

Special events on the hockey calendar help shape the outreach program. In 1987, for example, the Hall travelled outside of Toronto for the Rendez-vous series between NHL All Stars and the Soviet Union in Quebec City. Not only did this event bring a significant portion of the museum's collection to a new audience, but it also shaped the Hall's role in celebrating hockey on an international stage.

Thanks to new communications technology, the Hall has recently taken its outreach to outer space, using satellite feeds to communicate virtually in real time with schools in Canada's North and bring the Hall's collection to young people directly in their classrooms. *(Please see page 55 for more on this program.)*

The Hall ventured outside of Toronto in 1987 for an exhibition at the Rendez-vous Series between NHL All Stars and the U.S.S.R. The series, and exhibit, were a great success.

WALLEYE, BEARS AND BATS

Many artifacts in the Hall's collection find their way to the museum — from the minor leagues and the junior ranks, and even from schools — adding to the curiosity, and fun, of the collection.

Two East Coast Hockey League (now the ECHL) teams tapped into fans' pop culture interests to create a unique promotion in a November 2014 game. The Toledo Walleye and the Evansville Icemen competed on "Heroes Night," which celebrated the 75th anniversary of Batman. As the home team, the Walleye wore commemorative Batman jerseys while the visiting Icemen donned Riddler jerseys *(please see page 107)*. This mix of local hockey fervour, pop culture and marketing resulted in a unique experience for those in attendance and allowed the Hall to add a non-traditional artifact to its collection.

While the most prestigious hockey records are recorded in the NHL, the Hall's collection also celebrates important milestones and accomplishments that occur on innumerable levels of competition. The Hall's Westgate shares how they received the jersey, stick, two goal pucks and game sheet from a Junior A game on February 21, 1997, as well as newspaper articles chronicling the unusual exploit of Muskoka

Ryan Venturelli scored two unassisted goals in a Junior A game in 1997. His jersey and a few game artifacts made it into the collection. The catch? He scored them as a goalie.

79

THE GREATEST COLLECTION

Star material. Sidney Crosby's prep school jersey is on display at the Hall, as is Zach Parise's. They wore the same number, and very same jersey, while starring for Shattuck-St. Mary's School in Minnesota.

Bears goaltender Ryan Venturelli during it. Astonishingly, Venturelli scored two unassisted goals in one game, a feat which has likely never occurred in hockey history. Another set of artifacts from a Junior A is also on display. In 1999, the Markham Waxers donated BJ Forsyth's jersey and stick after the goaltender recorded six assists in one game. A popular jersey in the collection comes from Shattuck-St. Mary's School in tiny Faribault, MN, which happened to be worn both by Zach Parise and Sidney Crosby as teenagers. Each of these artifacts reinforces the Hall's goal and purpose of celebrating the sport as a whole. And while not everyone can be enshrined as Honoured Members, in some cases individual accomplishments can be showcased alongside the game's greats.

CHAPTER 6 | 'THE GOAL WAS ASSISTED BY...'

The Hall's publications collection is among the most extensive in hockey, including the first Hall of Fame book in print, along with popular annual programs.

HOCKEY CHRONICLES

Since 1961, the Hall has devoted itself to sharing its collected knowledge through books, special features in magazines, on television and through digital discussions. Bobby Hewitson tirelessly worked on creating the first Hall of Fame book to send both to hockey dignitaries and to sell to the public. Cyclone Taylor shared with the curator how this work helped teach hockey history to a new generation. "I have a couple of grandsons," the hockey legend wrote on January 12, 1962, "just getting interested in sports and I feel sure their grandmother gave them each one of my books." While not directly stated, Cyclone's message emphasized the purpose of Hewitson's tedious and tiresome effort to gather information on Honoured Members. The game's past, whether through the written word or physical artifacts or personal contact with a pioneer, connects present and future generations to the game's roots, origins and development.

Major publicity campaigns have also resulted in surges of interest for the Hall's publications. As Hewitson wrote to Clarence Campbell on December 9, 1963, a feature on "a coast to coast television show from Maple Leaf Gardens" resulted in a response that few expected "would be so large." In this letter, the curator shared that the shrine only had 360 books remaining, had sold 2,025 during the Canadian National Exhibition, and moved another 1,300 to people writing in requesting to purchase a book. As a result of the immense interest in hockey history, Campbell agreed that 1,000 more copies should be ordered. It's clear the Hall's publications have offered an effective vehicle to share hockey history with interested readers.

A GOOD REID

As the Hall's artifact collection and library continued to grow, so did the initial soft cover, stapled publication that Hewitson began putting together in 1961, which topped at 80 pages in 1968. The spiral-bound second version, *Hockey's Heritage* edited by Lefty Reid, lasted from 1969 through 1982. From 1983 through 1992, no formal annual publication existed outside of Induction Ceremony programs. Notably, in 1987

81

THE GREATEST COLLECTION

Two Rons. President Ronald Reagan was a big supporter of hockey in the U.S. He's shown greeting Ron Duguay of the New York Rangers.

a special edition of *Hockey's Heritage* was published in conjunction with the only Induction Ceremony held outside of Canada. For the special event in Detroit, several notable American dignitaries wrote introductions.

U.S. President Ronald Reagan echoed the Hall's mission and purpose by noting "induction into the Hall of Fame comes only to a few players, executives, and officials of outstanding capability, performance and commitment to the sport. Hockey Hall of Fame selectees are a fine example for aspiring hockey players everywhere." The president properly recognized that being chosen as an Honoured Member remains the exclusive domain of key individuals who have played at the highest levels of competition. The Hall's outreach to the U.S. and the publication of the sport's and shrine's history, however, allowed the museum to reach a much larger, diverse and untapped audience.

Once the Hall moved to their present location at Brookfield Place in Toronto's downtown, annual publications resumed. From 1993 through 2002, the *Yearbook* offered an assortment of articles on hockey history, descriptions of the Hall's exhibits, and detailed lists of Honoured Members. Beginning in 2003 and continuing through 2019, *Legends* followed a format similar to the *Yearbooks'*. Each *Legends* issue now chronicles key acquisitions from the previous year, many of which did not come from a National Hockey League player or team. Each year, through new articles, knowledge and collections, the Hall reconnects with an audience desiring to learn more about hockey history.

In the 1980s, the Hall not only shared history, but also added to how fans interact with the game's past when it partnered with a company named Cartophilium to produce an expansive trading card set. In September 1983, Reid shared with Johnny Bucyk that "the artist is Carlton McDiarmid, a professional artist in Montreal, who is also coincidentally a goal judge at The Forum for NHL games. So you can see that he has a genuine interest and knowledge of the game and its

A 1987 special card set featured all Honoured Members inducted to that point.

players." In 1983, the Hall released a 240-card set in both a postcard and traditional trading card format. By 1987, it decided to update the trading card set to include the 21 additional Honoured Members from the 1984 through '87 induction classes, bringing the total set size to 261. Because hockey card sets began being produced in 1910 and often only include players, these trading card sets include over 100 Honoured Members' first cards, including the game's earliest players, builders and officials who would otherwise be absent.

RINK RATS AND CULTURE VULTURES

The Hall also annually travels to major hockey events and tournaments. This tradition now dates back 20-plus years, illustrating the shrine's continual efforts to reach out to hockey fans. Whether the Hall produces exhibits for the World Junior Championship, the Memorial Cup, NHL All-Star Games, AHL All-Star Games, ECHL All-Star Games and the NHL Awards, the objective is the same: To share the game far and wide.

GREAT CONNECTION

Honoured Members themselves have been known to express appreciation for the Hall's collection. Regarding the Hall's special trading card set, Builder Carl Voss excitedly hand wrote to Lefty Reid on July 26, 1983, that it "is a great idea and undoubtedly will serve to create increased interest in the Hockey Hall of Fame at every level." He added that he had "interest" in obtaining dozens of copies of his own card and wished for Reid's "continual success as Curator of the Hockey Hall of Fame and also for the Hall of Fame card service project." Similar to the Hall's earlier efforts to gather data, collect artifacts and distribute programs chronicling the sport's and museum's history and membership, the card set formed another outreach effort that permitted fans and collectors to interact with the game's history and the Hall.

The electric green helmet Buddy Smith wore while representing the Arkansas RiverBlades in the 2003 ECHL All-Star Game adds a bit of minor league colour to the collection.

THE GREATEST COLLECTION

The Hall of Fame's Outreach Program impressively includes full displays of artifacts that pop up at virtually all major events around the hockey world.

FREQUENT FLYER PROGRAM

The Hockey Hall of Fame's Outreach Program is quite robust with the Hall regularly staging between four and eight events per month. (The frequency increases when the Stanley Cup is included in the mix.)

Many of these events are individual ones like the Pacific National Exhibition, the IIHF World Championship, the BATC Games in Saskatchewan, CIS University Cup (Now U Sports), Canadian National Championships such as the RBC Cup, Telus Cup, Esso Women's Nationals, Allan Cup, Canada Winter Games and various leagues' outdoor games. NHL Draft Parties and jersey number retirement nights are also popular stops, as well as various museum loans that showcase hockey.

These events are not limited to North America: The Hall's reach regularly extends around the globe as well, and over the years the Outreach Program has been tailored for exhibits in Germany, the Czech Republic, Switzerland, Hungary, Hong Kong, China, Australia, Great Britain, Russia and Kazakhstan, among many other nations.

The Outreach Program has grown in recent years to include displays, interactive games (mobile versions of the museum's popular Showdown and ShutOut challenges that test shooters and goalies), trophies and artwork. While no substitute for an actual visit to the Hall itself, the program provides fans who couldn't otherwise make it to Toronto with an opportunity to enjoy some of the game's great artifacts and memories.

CHAPTER 6 | 'THE GOAL WAS ASSISTED BY...'

The Hall regularly sends artifacts out on loan to help tell the story of teams like the Ottawa Senators, through a display at old City Hall, and the Edmonton Oilers, dramatically depicted in the media room at Rogers Arena.

ARTIFACT ROADSHOW

A successful part of the Hall's Outreach Program includes visiting communities with a mobile exhibit that features key items from the collection. Over the years, the travelling show and tell has made it to every NHL city — most recently as part of the league's centennial celebration in 2017 — and can regularly be found at NHL All-Star Games as part of the festivities. On the grassroots level, the exhibit has also been featured at charity events, tournaments and fundraisers in support of hockey communities everywhere.

As part of the visit, the Hall's curation team extends an open invitation to fans to bring hockey memorabilia for appraisal and possible inclusion into the collection as a donation. This can include game-worn jerseys or equipment, photos and collectibles that can have an important connection to the history of the game. The effort has resulted in numerous artifacts being added to the museum's permanent collection since the 1990s.

"One of the most interesting artifacts we have received from Outreach is a rug made from Detroit Red Wings sweaters (the equipment manager/trainer from the Red Wings used to bring the old sweaters home in the 1940s for his mom to take apart and make into rugs). We have them in our collection," said Phil Pritchard, Vice-President, Resource Centre and Curator, Hockey Hall of Fame.

"One of my favourites was in Prince Albert, SK, while at an anniversary celebration for the (Prince Albert) Raiders Memorial Cup and Centennial Cup teams," explained Izak Westgate, Outreach Exhibits and Assistant Curator. "In meeting the players, we managed to get a sweater from both championship teams, which filled holes for those eras in our collection."

For more information on how the Hall uncovers artifacts, please see page 116, Hockey Detectives.

THE GREATEST COLLECTION

In a few unique cases, the Hall and its hockey content jump the boards into the art world, where storytelling and visual presentation tend to follow a similar game plan as hockey displays. *The Power Play: Hockey in Canadian Contemporary Art* exhibition, for example, debuted at the Art Gallery of Windsor in 2019 under the direction of Curator Jaclyn Meloche, who initially contacted the Hall to ask if it would be willing to assist in building the exhibit.

Power Play, through the work of its participating artists, raises economic, political, gender and social questions related to the sport, expanding the narrative beyond NHL accomplishments. The Hall contributed key artifacts to this effort, including two Bev Beaver sweaters *(please see page 51)*, her hockey bag, and one of her MVP awards; a Gordie Howe cereal box and a Jacques Plante mask. These artifacts were combined with artistic interpretations of the game's impact. The powerful and stimulating collection is scheduled to tour Canada over several years, connecting hockey, and the Hall's collection, to new audiences in a unique way.

During the NHL's Centennial celebration in 2017, the Hall contributed artifacts and content to a travelling exhibition that visited every NHL city. This continental showcase allowed the museum to share hockey history with innumerable fans. These exhibits, whether in large formal campaigns or individual displays visiting a community, are a major manifestation of the Hall's efforts to highlight participation and enjoyment by recreational, youth, amateur and professional athletes and fans.

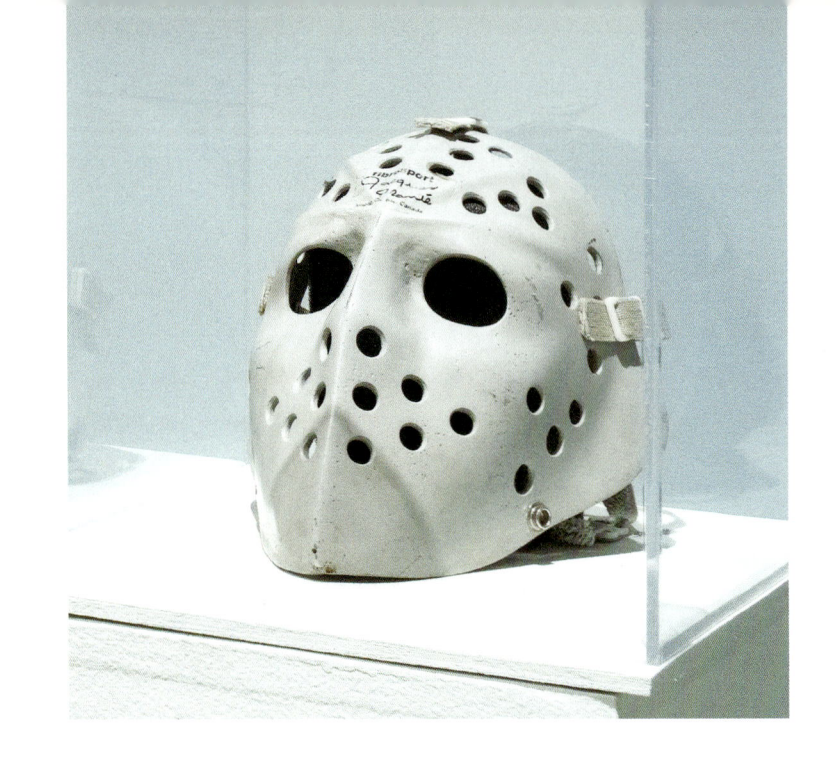

CHAPTER 6 | 'THE GOAL WAS ASSISTED BY...'

The 2019 Power Play: Hockey in Canadian Contemporary Art exhibition featured several key pieces form the Hall's collection, ranging from one of Jacques Plante's masks to a cereal box featuring "Mr. Hockey" to artifacts from Bev Beaver's career. *Power Play* also showcased works like a Jean-Paul Riopelle-inspired mural, with hockey cards substituting for paint.

GREAT CONNECTION

The Halll of Fame regularly works with other museums to tell the story of hockey. These are just some examples from recent years.

- 9/11 Museum | 2018-19
- Kalamazoo Valley Museum | 2018-19
- Pantheon des Sports de Québec | 2018-19
- Canadian Museum of History | 2018-19
- Canadian War Museum | 2017-18
- Museum of the City of New York | 2017-18
- Montreal Canadiens Museum
- Orillia Museum of Art & History | 2017-18
- City of Ottawa | 2017-18
- Pointe-à-Callière | 2017-18
- Waterloo Region Museum | 2017-18
- Manitoba Sports Hall of Fame (Sawchuk Mask) | 2014-15
- Museums of Burlington | 2015-16
- Canadian Museum of Immigration at Pier 21 | 2014-Current

FEATURED ARTIFACT

THE DETROIT RUG WINGS. IF YOU LOOK CLOSELY, REALLY, REALLY CLOSE, YOU MAY SEE A SWEATER OF A FAVOURITE 1940s RED WINGS PLAYER IN THIS RUG. THE MOM OF THE TEAM'S EQUIPMENT MANAGER AND TRAINER WOULD WEAVE THE WELL-WORN WINGED WHEEL WOOL INTO DECORATIVE COVERINGS.

AMONG THE MOST INTERESTING ARTIFACTS IN THE COLLECTION, THEY BECAME PART OF THE HALL'S TAPESTRY THROUGH ITS OUTREACH PROGRAM.

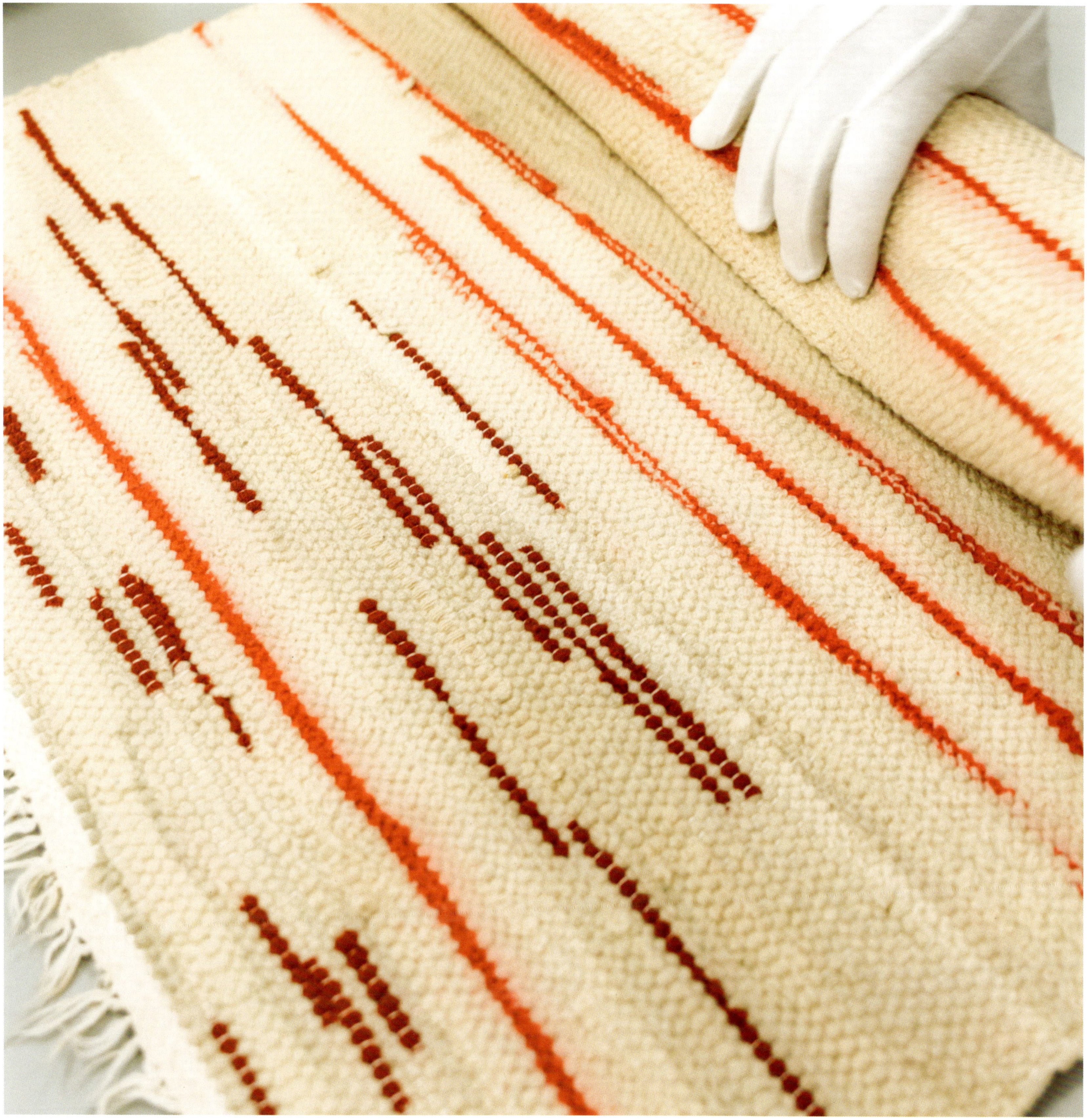

THE GREATEST COLLECTION

CHAPTER 7
THE GLOBAL GAME
Hockey's Ultimate Road Trip

There are a few handy tips to keep in mind when navigating the expansive Hockey Hall of Fame museum.

When you see the big bronze of children engaged in a hockey game in front of the most handsome historic building in downtown Toronto, you've arrived. The major trophies — including the "you know what" — are in the Great Hall. (Just follow the crowds.) And you'll know you're in the fantastic World of Hockey Zone that celebrates the game's global expansion when you see the famous red jersey of the Soviet Union from its first World Championship team in 1954. Right?

Wrong. The "Big *Red* Machine's" first sweater was blue.

And therein lies another tip for pilgrims to hockey's shrine: expect the unexpected. As much as the Holy Grail Stanley Cup and other major icons excite and enthral, it's the small curiosities like the CCCP blue sweater on display that make the Hall's collection so interesting, especially in the telling of the game's international expansion.

CMYK...and heavy on the cyan. The U.S.S.R. national team sweater from 1954 was a striking blue, not the menacing red opponents would come to fear.

International Ice Hockey Federation

An early display at the CNE features numerous artifacts from International Ice Hockey Federation member teams.

AN EVOLVING REVOLVING EXHIBIT

The opening of the World of Hockey exhibit in 1998 reinforced the Hall's quest to commemorate the game wherever it's played. This expansion represented the first major addition to the displays and occurred after collaborating with the International Ice Hockey Federation (IIHF) and in conjunction with the Winter Olympic Games. John MacKinnon, the Canadian Hockey Association's manager of communications, recognized in the 1998 *Yearbook* that "ice hockey long ago ceased to be the private preserve" of Canadians. Rather than focusing on Canada's greatness, he instead described how the game brings joy to people all around the world. MacKinnon argued that, whether "most North Americans realize it or not, [hockey] energizes people in places as seemingly unlikely as Thailand, South Africa, Israel, Australia, and Greece."

While the Hall's mandate to celebrate the history and development of hockey has never wavered, its ability to display the ever-expanding world game in a world-class way was made possible through the 1993 move to BCE Place (now Brookfield Place) in downtown Toronto. The additional exhibition space and a growing collection allowed the museum to include more non-traditional perspectives in the narrative through the creation of The International Zone, an exhibit, according to John Armstrong in the 1993 *Yearbook*, that included "thirty-two countries from around the world" in order to tell the history of international hockey.

Visitors could now experience international competition through artifacts and the use of technology. In an effort to include as many groups as possible, "games from nine different countries [could] be viewed on monitors, accompanied by play-by-play commentary in English, French or the language of the host country." By integrating these aspects, especially the interactive features, the Hall could showcase international tournaments and explain the role national teams have played in the growth of hockey around the world.

THE GREATEST COLLECTION

The Hall of Fame collection features artifacts from everywhere hockey is played. The South African Springbok jersey is a great example of team colours and imagery from one of hockey's "hotbeds."

CHAPTER 7 | THE GLOBAL GAME

Teemu Selanne was one of the most beloved stars in international hockey. He was a fan favourite wherever he played, including Winnipeg, Anaheim and his native Finland. The "Finnish Flash" favoured his nation's equipment, in this case Jofa elbow pads he used during the 2006-07 season and playoffs.

BUILD IT AND THEY WILL KOMME/KOMMA/KOMMEN SIE

The decision to grow global content at the Hall would pay dividends, and quickly. Federations, leagues and participants from around the world were eager to participate and happy to be represented at first in the International Zone and then the World of Hockey exhibit. Today, the 6,000-square-foot area is the largest exhibit space dedicated to one subject in the entire museum. For many visitors either from foreign nations or with international heritage to the Hall, their home nation has been represented in displays, which further fulfills the Hall's effort to celebrate the game's widespread reach.

In addition to featuring nearly 200 members of the International Ice Hockey Hall of Fame, the display area celebrates members of the Triple Gold Club (players who have won the Stanley Cup, World Championships and Olympic Gold) who have cemented their reputations as true international stars, and has further developed interactive features with the Global Game Flight Deck. More than 75 different International Ice Hockey Federation member nations are now represented, a clear indication of how hockey has expanded to all the corners of the Earth. Of course, the bigger hockey powers in North America and Europe are well represented, but so are less-traditional hockey hotbeds such as South Africa and Lebanon, each contributing to the overarching narrative of hockey's influence. The collection of terrific team jerseys from some of the junior hockey nations, featuring great colours and great logos, are alone worth the price of admission.

Non-North American participation in hockey at all levels has rapidly increased over the decades. Sweden, Finland and Slovakia have all produced hockey icons. The Czech Republic burst onto the international scene by winning the 1998 Olympic gold medal, the first tournament in which NHL players could participate. Jaromir Jagr and Dominik Hasek, whose national team game-used jersey now is part of the Hall's collection, helped the nation surpass traditional favourites like Canada, the United States and Russia.

THE GREATEST COLLECTION

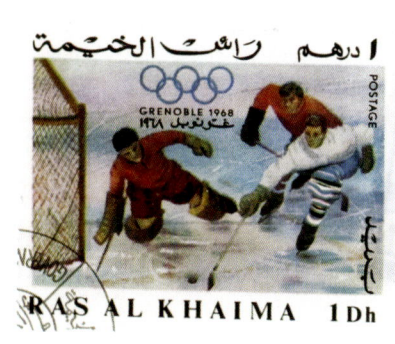

The stamps in the Hall's collection celebrate the beauty of hockey wherever it's played, and also signature moments that dominate the history of international competition.

HOCKEY HALL OF PHILATELY

There are plenty of items on display at the Hall that tell of the expansion of hockey as a global game. In fact, the international exhibits are some of the biggest and most popular at the museum, showcasing everything from national team jerseys to Olympic medals to international trophies to at least one charmed coin. The exhibits also feature some of the smallest, albeit hard-working in the collection in terms of spreading the joy of hockey — postage stamps.

The humble stamp, the greatest traveller the world has ever known, has been carrying the mail when it comes to international correspondence since its rookie year in 1840. From the outset, stamps would feature an image related to the issuing country, connecting it with a famous person, setting or event, for example, and capturing the greater spirit of the subject within the tiniest of windows. In turn, the stamps themselves would capture the imagination of hobbyists who made collecting a pastime shared by countless millions, including the Hall of Fame whose collection features an intriguing variety of paid postage spanning continents and decades.

The stamps in the Hall's collection depict hockey as an action-filled sport no matter where it's played, whether outdoors or in, and from the pond to the pinnacle of World Championships and Olympiads. They include classic interpretations of the game from international artists and highlight specific moments of national pride.

All in a postage stamp-sized format.

CHAPTER 7 | THE GLOBAL GAME

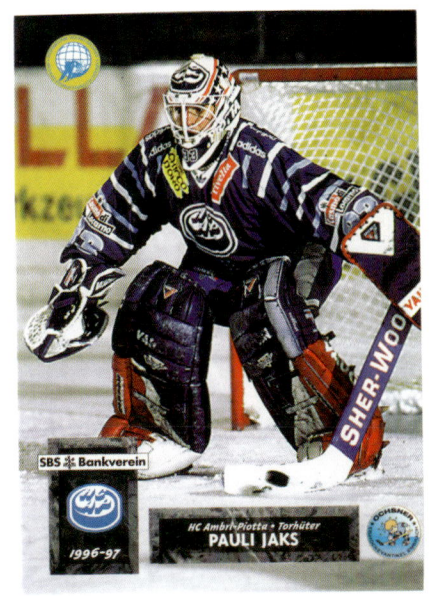

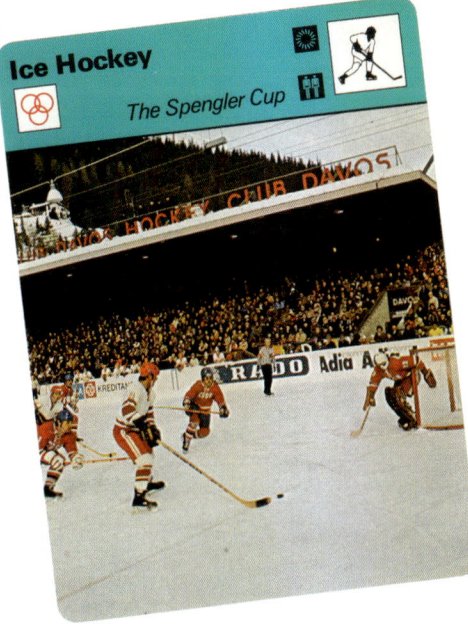

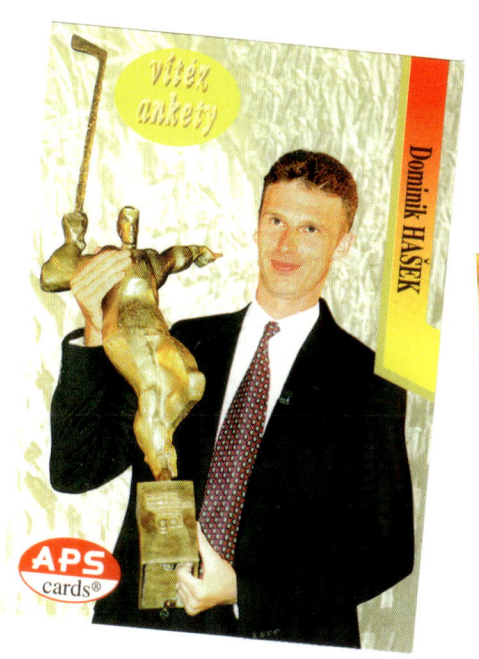

Like the stamps on the facing pages, hockey cards the world over depict famous players and memorable moments on the international stage.

INTERNATIONAL HOCKEY CARDS

In much the same way the Hockey Hall of Fame's vast collection showcases hockey wherever it is played, trading cards (please see Personal Treasures, page 60) are not limited to celebrating North American players — nor are they limited to English.

Many of the world's leading hockey countries, including, Sweden, Finland, the Czech Republic/Czechoslovakia and Russia, to name a few, have their own hockey heritage depicted on cards. These cards are often written, sometimes exclusively, in the nation's native language and offer more culturally correct spellings of players' names.

For example, many of the Honoured Members in the Hall who played for the U.S.S.R. (CCCP) have early European issued cards. Alexander Yakushev (Alexander Jakusjev), Vladislav Tretiak (Vladislav Trejak) and Valeri Kharlamov (Valerij Kharlamov), are all Cyrillically commemorated on cardboard, each a household name in his native Russia as much as in North America.

These international cards and sets provide fans an opportunity to add a certain accent to their personal collections by trading for pieces of history and celebrating the international game's greatest players. For the Hockey Hall of Fame, a significant card collector in its own right, the opportunity is to not only share the story of the game, but also provide a glimpse into the culture of some of hockey's great nations.

COOL BRITANNIA

As much as the Czech Republic gold in '98 was a surprise of sorts, given the stiff competition of the Olympic tournament that year, it wasn't a shocker on the level that upstart Great Britain delivered 62 years earlier against powerhouse Canada.

From the outset of Olympic play in 1924, Canada had exerted its hockey dominance, winning consecutive gold medals in three straight winter Games (and four in a row if you count its 1920 win at the *Summer* Olympics in Antwerp!) And then came 1936 and the greatest upset in international hockey history to that point in time.

Great Britain, creatively constructing their team with Canadian-raised-and-trained players who were mostly British born, upset the dominant Canucks 2-1 at Garmisch-Partenkirchen, Germany, before moving on to capture the nation's first and only gold medal.

The shocking triumph has had a lasting impact. When British-born J.F. "Bunny" Ahearne, the former President of the International Ice Hockey Federation, was inducted into the shrine as a Builder in 1977, he added a unique perspective on hockey history. As he wrote to Lefty Reid on September 30, 1977, he noted how "details of the British Ice Hockey Association will be worked out in the near future and I will have great pleasure in sending you a copy as promised." Implicit in this comment was that Britain had its own hockey heritage (in fact, it was a founding member of the IIHF in 1908) and that information regarding this enjoyment could add to the Hall's efforts to convey hockey's global reach.

GREAT BRITAIN
Olympic Champions—1936

Standing—left to right: J. F. AHEARNE (Secretary, B.I.H.A.) and Team Manager, J. CHAPPELL A. ST
G. DAILLEY P. NICKLIN (Coach) J. KILPATRICK J. FOSTER J. COWARD G. DAVEY P. V. HU
Kneeling—left to right: R. WYMAN J. BORLAND A. CHILD E. BRENCHLEY
Not included is C. ERHARDT (Team Captain)

CHAPTER 7 | THE GLOBAL GAME

The upstart Brits surprised the hockey world with their gold medal win at the 1936 Olympics. Their classic national team sweater is shown.

97

THE GREATEST COLLECTION

STARS OF THE SUMMER GAMES

Hockey made its Olympic debut at Antwerp, Belgium, in 1920. It was the Summer Games. (The Winter Olympics, which included hockey, were first played in 1924.) The season wasn't the only curiosity surrounding the tournament.

Seven teams would compete in 1920 at the Palais de Glace d'Anvers (Antwerp ice palace), with seven players per side, including a rover. The rink was smaller than North American standards, roughly 184 by 59 feet, the opposite of the current situation, in which the International game is played on a bigger (wider) ice surface than in the NHL.

Canada dominated play and won the gold medal in 1920, allowing just a single goal against throughout the competition. The country was represented by club team Winnipeg Falcons of the Manitoba Hockey League, which was made up mainly of players of Icelandic descent. The team had overcome obstacles in its early days. These included racial prejudice owing to the players' heritage; war — seven of eight members enlisted to fight in the First World War in which two were killed; and on-ice battles — including against rivals from the Winnipeg Hockey League. It still won Olympic gold.

The Winnipeg Falcons' team sweater and gold medal from the 1920 Olympics are prized artifacts in the Hall's collection.

98

CHAPTER 7 | THE GLOBAL GAME

Photos from the 1920 Olympics show the original national teams that helped bring hockey to the world stage.

99

THE GREATEST COLLECTION

Coach, author and Father of Russian hockey Anatoli Tarasov left his mark on the world game. He was recognized for his many accomplishments when he was inducted into the Hall in 1974, the first Russian to be so honoured.

BIG RED'S BIG IMPACT

Two decades after the British victory, the Soviet Union emerged as a formidable threat to North American hockey greatness with its first world title in 1954. Their success would not be as fleeting. The Big Red Machine would dominate international hockey for more than 30 years, bringing a level of precision and speed to the game previously not seen. Indeed, their national team CCCP red sweaters — the blue blip at the Hall notwithstanding — would strike fear in the hearts of opponents en route to 22 World Championships between 1954-90, and seven Olympic golds through 1988.

As Cyclone Taylor wrote to Bobby Hewitson on December 31, 1964, "these Russians certainly deserve a good deal of credit in taking into [competition] our best Hockey teams all across Canada. They play very nice Hockey, it reminds me very much of the style played some years ago." Anatoli Tarasov's *Road to Olympus* book in the Hall's collection provides critical insight into how the Russian learned and adapted the Canadian game to become a power on the international stage.

Tarasov, "the father of Russian hockey," is celebrated at the Hall for his contributions to hockey and described by writer Milt Dunnell as being "one of the most progressive and dedicated exponents in the world." All told, Tarasov would lead the national team to nine straight World Championships and three Olympic gold medals. In 1974, the coaching legend became the first Russian enshrined in the Hall in the Builder category.

Today, the memory of the Soviet Union's success on the international stage, as well as the highly contested Summit Series in 1972 has resulted in a romanticization of the Cold War sporting contests. Additionally, Soviet players who never played for a North American league or team have achieved enshrinement, including Vladislav Tretiak (1989), Valeri Kharlamov (2005) and Aleksander Yakushev (2018). They are now cornerstones in the Hall's efforts to tell a global narrative of hockey and the Russian influence on the game, beginning with the national team and later extending to players starring in the NHL. It's

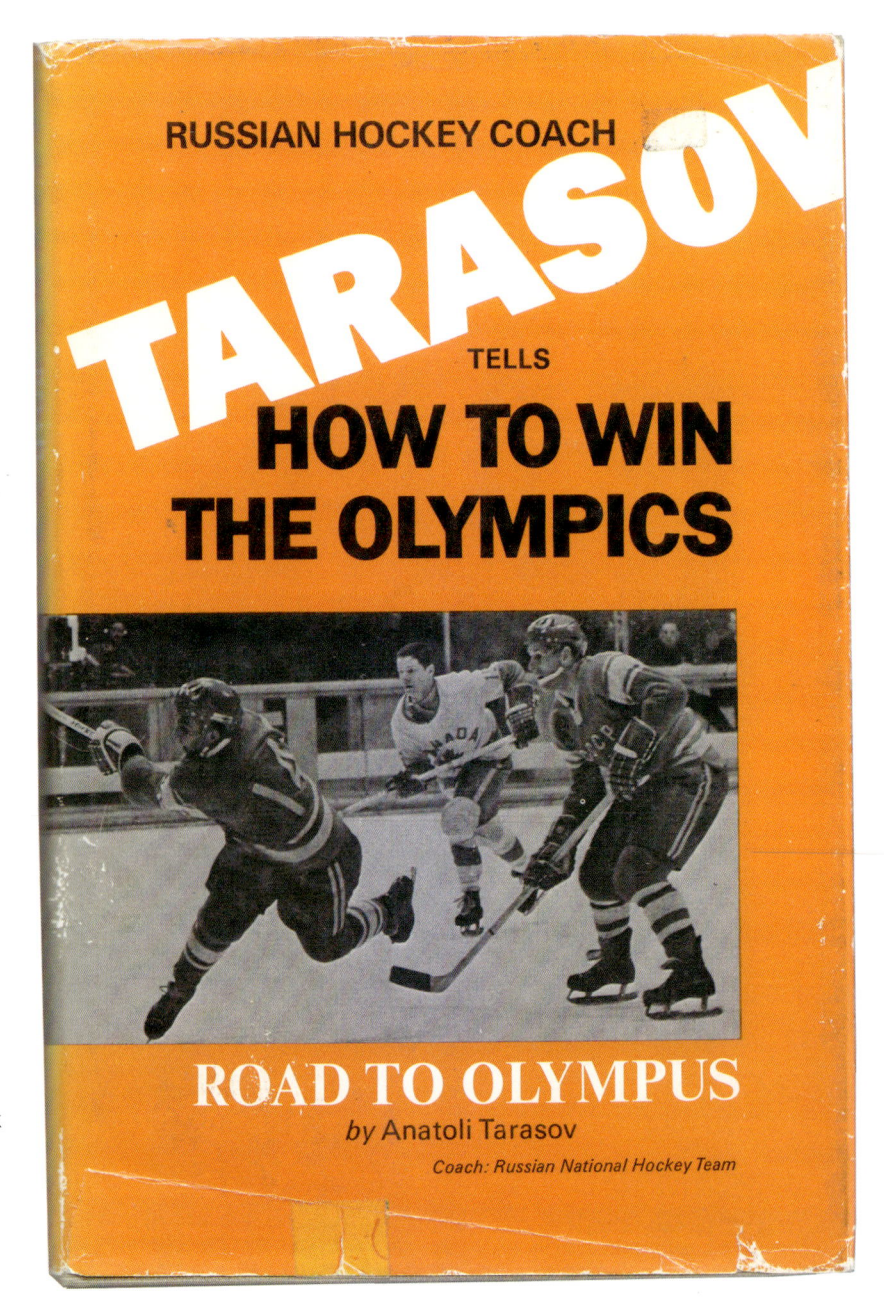

100

CHAPTER 7 | THE GLOBAL GAME

GREAT CONNECTION

Though the Hall always desired to be an international institution, limited exhibition space and hockey's gradual growth initially resulted in the museum's narrative being restricted to North America and strong hockey nations like Sweden and Russia. Over time, outreach programs helped spread the sport across the globe, creating a common interest despite the differences in politics, language and culture. The Hall stresses this uniting force, celebrating hockey as a common interest that allows participants, spectators and interested individuals to associate with the game's history and values.

fitting that Russia and the Soviet Union are prominently represented in the Word of Hockey beginning with Tretiak and his enshrinement as the first player born and trained outside of North America to be inducted as an Honoured Member. Bill Hay, the future chairman of the Hall, summed up the nomination of the goaltending great and latter-day statesman eloquently.

"Tretiak has been a motivating force," he argued, "not only while playing competitively, but also as an ambassador for the game in elevating the standard of international play for not only the amateurs but for the pros as well."

The Hall will continue to mark the march of hockey across the globe and to honour the stars and pioneers who blaze new trails for the game, their stories told through an even greater collection.

"Tretiak has been a motivating force," he argued, "not only while playing competitively, but also as an ambassador for the game…"

Tarasov was a trailblazer who built Russia's Big Red Machine into the most impressive national team in the world, their talents on full display during the 1972 Summit Series against Canada.

FEATURED ARTIFACT

THE EDINBURGH TROPHY MAY NOT BE THE MOST POPULAR CHAMPIONSHIP ARTIFACT IN THE HALL'S COLLECTION, BUT IT'S AMONG ITS MOST BEAUTIFUL.

IT WAS PRESENTED TO THE WINNERS OF A SERIES PLAYED BETWEEN THE CHAMPIONS OF THE WESTERN HOCKEY LEAGUE AND THE QUEBEC HOCKEY LEAGUE BETWEEN 1954-57. IT WAS DONATED BY PRINCE PHILIP, DUKE OF EDINBURGH, AND FEATURES A SILVER HOCKEY PLAYER MOUNTED ON TOP OF A SILVER GLOBE.

THE GLOBE IS ATTACHED TO A BLACK EBONY BASE WITH THE COAT OF ARMS OF THE DOMINION OF CANADA. THE WINNERS WERE TO BE CONSIDERED THE WORLD'S MINOR PROFESSIONAL CHAMPIONS.

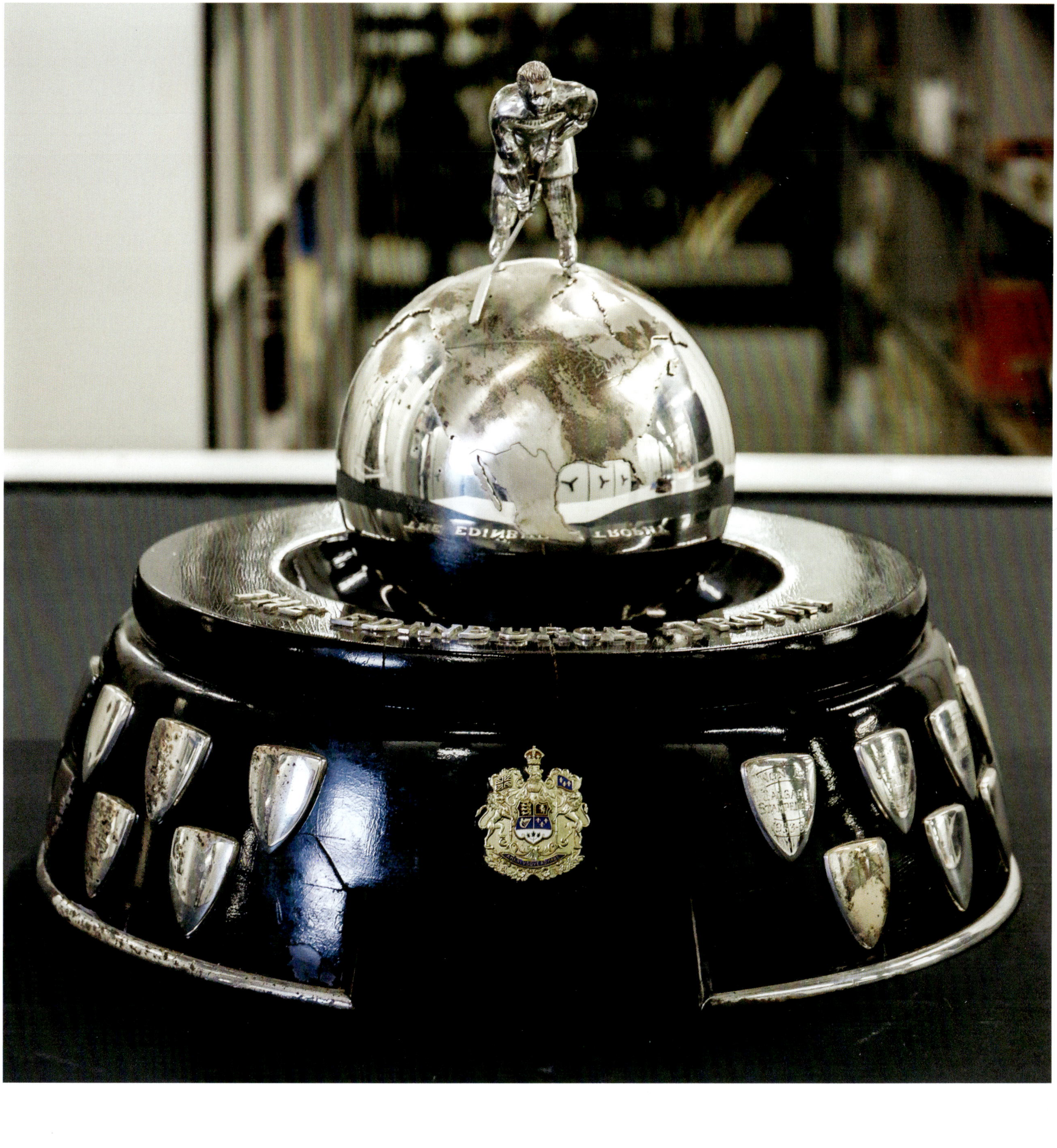

THE GREATEST COLLECTION

CHAPTER 8
'BEST GAME YOU CAN NAME'
Hockey and Pop Culture

"Hello out there, we're on the air, it's 'Hockey Night' tonight.

"Tension grows, the whistle blows, and the puck goes down the ice. The goalie jumps, and the players bump, and the fans all go insane. Someone roars, Bobby Scores!, at the good ol' Hockey Game.

"Oh! The good ol' Hockey game, is the best game you can name. And the best game you can name, is the good ol' Hockey game."

- Stompin' Tom Connors, The Hockey Song

There couldn't be a better rallying cry to hockey nation than Stompin' Tom's ode to game night. It captures the action and spirit of the game and lays it out in simple country poetry. A standard in arenas everywhere, the song has also enjoyed wide radio play since its release in 1973 and has become the *de facto* anthem for the simple enjoyment of hockey. It's also a great example of how the game sometimes transcends athletics and enters the public imagination through pop culture, whether film, art or music — or at least one pinball machine.

WHO DOESN'T WANT TO DRIVE THE ZAMBONI?!
As part of its vast collection, the Hockey Hall of Fame has commemorated the sport's connection to pop culture and the unique ways in which fans' music, film and TV interests have interacted and intersected with hockey. In addition to the Hockey in Popular Culture exhibit in the *Upper Deck Collectors' Corner* from 2019 that seeks to offer a "glimpse at the way our game has been depicted in film, television, music, literature and more," the Hall stores both enormous and small mementos that showcase some of the ways fans have connected, collected and shaped the sport for decades.

Popular music has long-shaped the in-game experience on hockey nights. While music at games entertains fans with both traditional and popular numbers, songs about hockey bring the sport to a broader audience through concerts or radio play. One catchy tune from 1990 by the Gear Daddies went as far as popularizing a quintessential staple of hockey itself in the song, *I Wanna Drive the Zamboni*. The Hall has recognized the distinct association of the Zamboni and the sport and, as part of the Greatest Collection, acquired one of the machines that cleaned the ice at the Boston Garden. Originally, the museum proudly displayed this massive artifact at the entrance of the Hall of Fame in downtown Toronto with plans to return the ice cleaner to public display in a revamped Arena Zone that will also return other Original Six relics like the organ from Maple Leaf Gardens, ticket wickets and turnstiles to the exhibition floor.

SUPER POWERS
As following sports does, pop culture entertains, excites and unites. Personal memories and preferences allow for many, even diverse, groups to participate due to a common interest in a character, theme or project. Goalie masks are a great example. They provide a medium for athletes to share their passions and artistry, and to share the passion with fans. Ken Wregget's Pittsburgh Penguins mask from 1996-98

The Zamboni from the Boston Garden is the biggest artifact in the Hall's collection — a donation from the Big Bad Bruins.

105

THE GREATEST COLLECTION

CHAPTER 8 | 'BEST GAME YOU CAN NAME'

Hockey in pop culture has been a popular theme for a long time, as displayed in the Hall's eclectic collection of commercial memorabilia.

depicts Danny Devito as the Penguin from the 1992 *Batman Returns* movie. Whether or not a visitor actually recalls watching hockey when Wregget bore this iconic protection, the pop culture reference allows for a unique connection between sport and society. The Hall's vast collection of iconic masks allows viewers to not only see the game's evolution and development, but to also consider the personalities and interests of the players who wore the protective gear. Or just simply enjoy the art work that is unique to hockey.

Pop culture icons can be adapted in unique ways to tie in to hockey. Minor league hockey often creates fun promotions that directly connect to a community's interest. After an ECHL game on November 22, 2014, between the Toledo Walleye and Evansville Icemen, the Hall received two unique jerseys. As part of the superhero's 75th anniversary, the Toledo home team wore Batman jerseys while the Icemen wore opposing Riddler jerseys. For the fans in attendance and the visitors to the Hall, this elaborate presentation allowed for a fun and unique connection between beloved characters and a local franchise.

"I admire that in a man with a mask." The Penguin from the Batman series of movies was a logical choice for Ken Wregget's Pittsburgh Penguins goalie mask.

107

THE GREATEST COLLECTION

"When I arrived at the skating rink in my blue sweater all the Maurice Richards in red, white and blue came up, one by one, to take a look. When the referee blew his whistle I went to take my usual position. The coach came and warned me I'd be better to stay on the forward line… By the third period I still had not played…"

From The Hockey Sweater, by Roch Carrier

If you're a hockey fan, odds are you have at least one jersey, likely your hometown team's, hanging in your closet. Jerseys are the most common outward manifestation of loyalty shown by fans. Beyond sport, they express civic pride that, when shared by thousands upon thousands of likeminded supporters, bring together perfect strangers under a single, uniting identity. Multiply that by a thousand, and you'll probably begin to come close to what the red, white and blue and "CH" mean to followers of the Montreal Canadiens, especially among the team's French Canadian fanbase.

The Habs, short for the French *habitants*, are one of those unique franchises that have come to represent a people, sharing an identity beyond hockey itself. Language, culture and, at times, religion have all contributed to the identity of the hockey team whose jersey is worn with as much passion as it is pride. Imagine the horror, therefore, when, as a young boy, Roch Carrier opened a present one morning in 1946 and found not the sweater of his beloved Canadiens in the box, but the woollen sweater of rival Toronto Maple Leafs. Instead of keeping his misfortune under wraps, Carrier bravely wore the Leafs' blue and white down to the outdoor rink where he tried to join in a game with the other kids in his rural Quebec town, all of whom were decked out in fiery red Montreal sweaters with Maurice Richard's number 9 on the back. What transpired is a story best told by Carrier, which became one of the most popular children's books ever published in Canada. As for the object of the decorated author's affection, Richard's famous No. 9, it remains one of the most popular *chandails* in the Hall's collection (*please see page 111*).

Maurice "Rocket" Richard, more precisely, his sweater, shown in the photo from the 1946-47 season above, was the subject of Rock Carrier's famous children's book.

The Hall's Craig Campbell, left, and Phil Pritchard have the honour of handing out the Stanley Cup each year, as their likenesses depicted on this Playmobil toy.

GAMES, SOUVENIRS AND MEMENTOES

The connection between pop culture and hockey extends to symbols and events of many individuals' childhood memories. Prominently displayed in the *Upper Deck Collectors' Corner* sits a Bally Bobby Orr Power Play pinball machine from 1978. Reflecting the popularity of arcades in the late 20th century, the game used the name, prestige and appeal of No. 4's career to attract pinball enthusiasts.

Hockey also routinely reached into kids' daily routines. Mixed among cereal boxes, pennants and numerous other hockey trinkets in the *Upper Deck Collectors' Corner* sit two unique Wayne Gretzky collectibles from the 1980s. First, an Aladdin brand lunch box allows kids to share their fandom with their friends. A year later, Mattel created a Wayne Gretzky doll along with three accessory sets — an away sweater, a suit and a track suit. The pinball machine, the lunch box and the doll reflect how major companies used hockey to tap into expanding consumerism. The Hall's collection shows how superstars and legends would help use pop culture to reinforce fan interest outside of the arena.

During the 2014-15 season, Rapid City of the ECHL celebrated Dr. Seuss Night with special jerseys to the delight of every fan of the Rush...and their crush.

Wayne Gretzky's image was stamped on just about everything at one point, including school lunch boxes.

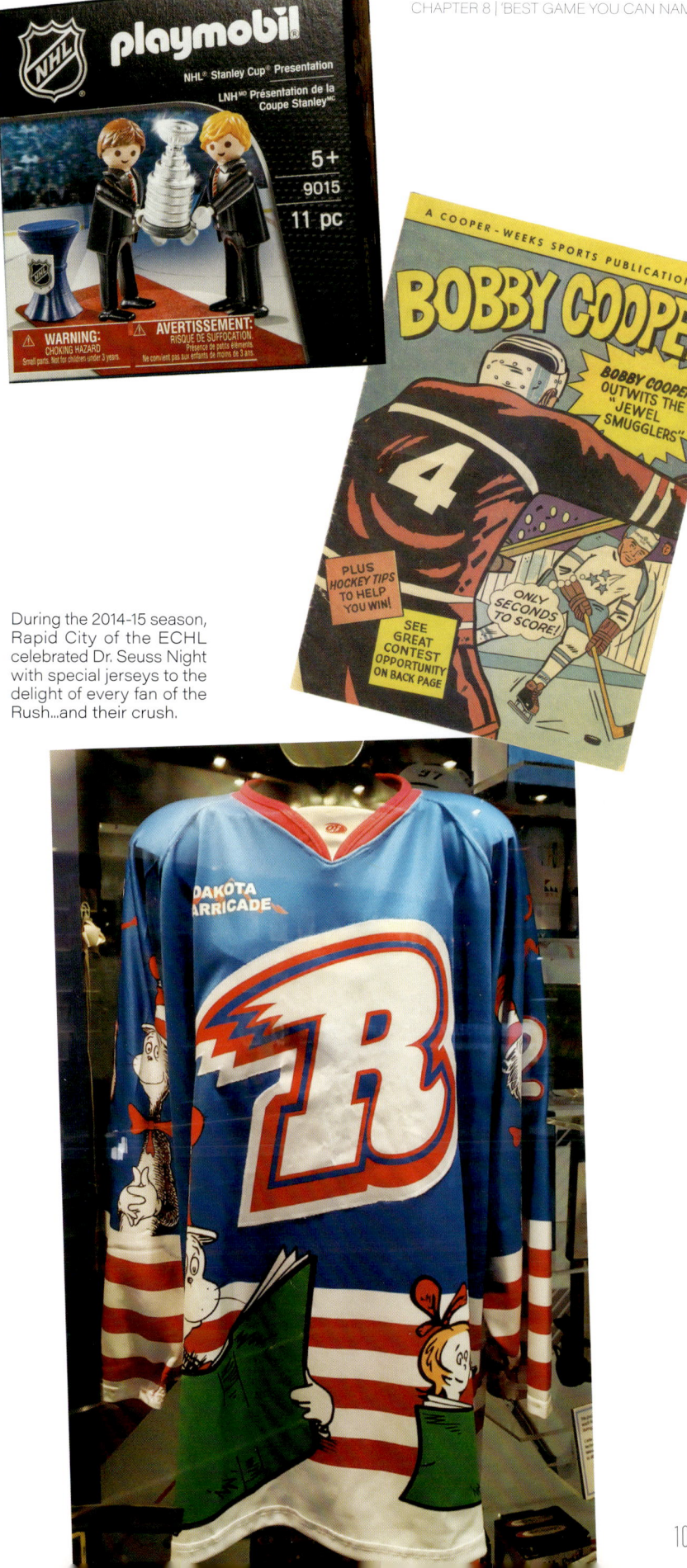

CHAPTER 8 | 'BEST GAME YOU CAN NAME'

109

THE GREATEST COLLECTION

Mask art oftentimes relates to pop art, including the designs of these two famous masks that were featured in the hockey movie *Youngblood*.

SAVING FACE, *REDUX*

It's a bit ironic that the most introspective player on any hockey team is typically the goalie, the same person who wears their emotions on their face — well, over their face — for all to see.

Goaltending mask art adds a sense of artistic flair to any hockey game. The protective gear has been transformed into Kevlar canvas that has come to reflect team identity, the goalie's personality or even to deliver a personal message, all through creative and increasingly elaborate artwork.

While playing for the Chicago Blackhawks, Honoured Member Ed Belfour wore a bold red mask with a screaming eagle on the sides, reflecting his nickname and aggressive play style. This striking imagery, which he also adapted for future masks while playing for the San Jose Sharks, Dallas Stars, Toronto Maple Leafs and Florida Panthers, became as closely associated with Belfour as his accomplishments on the ice.

Similarly, Brian Hayward's mask while playing for the San Jose Sharks offered an iconic and intimidating perspective for fans. The long-time Anaheim Ducks commentator peered through a cage surrounded by a menacing set of shark teeth with some blood dripping, suggesting a successful attack on an opposing player.

The Hall's exhibition of masks throughout history, from rudimentary protection with minimalist art to high-tech headgear with dynamic design, continues to be a fan-favourite attraction.

CHAPTER 8 | 'BEST GAME YOU CAN NAME'

Maurice Richard's sweater in the Hall's collection, shown, is a later version of the one featured in *The Hockey Sweater*. The captain's "C" first appeared on the Rocket's sweater in 1956.

NOT JUST ANY HOCKEY SWEATER

Roch Carrier could always blame his mom — to the extent that anyone would want to blame their mother for anything — for getting it wrong and having the Eaton department store deliver a Toronto Maple Leafs sweater to his Sainte-Justine, Quebec, home in the winter of 1946. He could also thank his mom for the error that would give rise to one of the most popular children's stories ever written — and not necessarily only for children.

The Hockey Sweater, Le Chandail de Hockey in its original French, at its heart is a simple and good story, according to the author himself. Reviewers, academics and social commentators, don't disagree, but add to the importance of the work by pointing to it as an allegory that speaks to a cultural and linguistic chasm, in this case between the English, represented by the Maple Leafs, and the French, reflected in *les Canadiens de Montréal*, of Canada. But it's a good story first, and hundreds of thousands of readers agree, as do film producers — it won an award for best animated film — the Prince of Wales — a copy was presented to him and his family as a gift — and to astronauts – the book has travelled to the International Space Station. It has also received numerous other accolades since being published in 1979, as has Carrier himself who was awarded the Order of Canada, one of the nation's highest honours, for the story and his overall body of work.

And then there are the French-language immersion schools that have been named after Carrier, symphony productions that dramatically feature *The Hockey Sweater* and countless readings to countless schools and youth groups over the years.

You can thank his mom for all of it.

THE GREATEST COLLECTION

Paul Newman played the lead as a fictional Chief, while some of his teammates in the film were actual professional hockey players.

The Ducks' jersey lacked its might in the Hollywood film, but the movie more than made up for it at the box office.

112

A MIGHTY IMPACT

*"Well Reg is our coach
Yeah, sure Old Time Hockey!
Like Eddie Shore
Eddie Shore yeah
Coach...our line starts?"*

-The Hanson Brothers, Slap Shot

Saying the movie *Slap Shot* enjoys a cult following among hockey fans is like saying NHLers would kinda' like to win the Stanley Cup. The film, which tells of the exploits of the fictional minor league Charlestown Chiefs, is the most popular hockey film of all time, and, by some accounts, the best sports movie ever made. It resonates with fans probably because it depicts what likely happened, and oftentimes did, in the rough and tumble minor leagues in the mid-1970s, with comic results. (That, and Paul Newman.)

Slap Shot was pretty much on point with its reference to Eddie Shore and "old time hockey." For the scrappy Bruins legend, there was no other kind. It also based the fictional Hansons on real life pro players the Carlson brothers, including Jack who played in the WHA and NHL and finished his career with the Minnesota North Stars in the 1986-87 season. He missed starring in the film alongside his siblings, Jeff and Steve, however, when he was called up to the big leagues prior to filming. His role would be filled by fellow pro Dave Hanson. The movie was a hit, garnering legions of fans, including the Hall of Fame, which regularly features *Slap Shot* memorabilia at the museum.

While the film set the standard for popular hockey flicks, another movie franchise directly impacted the NHL's expansion and inspired generations of future players.

GREAT CONNECTION

Hockey is most often enjoyed through television and radio broadcasts via play-by-play and commentary delivered by announcers and presenters, some of whom have created their own following over the years through memorable calls. The *TSN/RDS Broadcast Zone* at the Hall gives fans a shot at calling their own shot from behind a replica Sportscentre desk where they can sit in as sports anchor and fill in the audio for a famous hockey moment. The Hall records each take and encourages visitors to share them online. Warning: It's not as easy as the pros make it sound!

The tale of an underdog winning the "Pee Wee Championship" connected with and encouraged young hockey fans and players in the 1990s. "We all grew up" on the sports movies, Edmonton Oilers captain Connor McDavid recalled. California-born and Arizona-raised Auston Matthews rates *The Mighty Ducks* movie as his favourite sports film. Disney turned their fictional team name and logo into a successful NHL franchise. Though the entertainment company sold the team a few years after it reached the Stanley Cup Final in 2003, Henry and Susan Samueli would answer the duck call, eventually changing the team name to the Anaheim Ducks and bringing the first Stanley Cup to California in 2007.

The first ever draft pick of the Mighty Ducks of Anaheim was Paul Kariya. He's shown here on draft day with General Manager Pierre Gauthier.

FEATURED ARTIFACT

ANYONE FOR TEA? EVERYONE, ITS SEEMS, WANTED TO ALIGN THEIR CONSUMER PRODUCTS WITH NHLERS AT ONE POINT OR ANOTHER, INCLUDING SHIRRIFF SALADA, THE FOOD PRODUCTS COMPANY THAT PRODUCED COLLECTIBLE COINS FEATURING PLAYER IMAGES BEGINNING IN THE LATE 1950s.

THE COINS ARE STILL TRADED TO THIS DAY, INDIVIDUALLY AND BY SETS (TEAMS AND YEARS).

115

THE GREATEST COLLECTION

CHAPTER 9
HOCKEY DETECTIVES
To Protect and (Pre)Serve

"Just the facts, ma'am…"

Television fans of a certain age will recognize the catchphrase above from the popular police drama *Dragnet* and its lead character, fictional detective Joe Friday. It doesn't matter that the good sergeant didn't utter those exact words, viewers could count on his dogged pursuit of the truth to solve each episode's case in under 30 minutes.

While the Hockey Hall of Fame is not in the business of fighting crime, fictional or otherwise, its pursuit of the facts, in this case, artifacts, would make Detective Friday proud. He would certainly appreciate the police-like proficiency with which the staff of the Hall's Resource Centre pursues, acquires and confirms the authenticity of hockey's treasures no matter where in hiding they may be. It's a huge part of what makes The Greatest Collection great, but it's not a story that's widely known.

BADGE OF HONOUR

The staff at the Resource Centre, working under the expert guidance of Curator Phil Pritchard, prides itself on acquiring, preserving and sharing hockey history. To them, each artifact provides a unique perspective on the evolution of the sport. While the storage and public display of these items provide a direct connection between fans, visitors and museum, the process of shaping hockey history for permanent preservation requires tremendous work and dedication, as well as research, study and a bit of scientific ingenuity.

Resource Centre staff dedicate tremendous time and resources to ensure that artifacts are properly preserved, conserved and catalogued for posterity. As Curator Pritchard notes, "Each artifact is different and requires specialized care and individualized processes in order to most effectively conserve, store and display pieces of hockey history."

TAKEN INTO CUSTODY

Immediately upon taking possession of a newly acquired artifact, the Resource Centre staff will document it and send a copy of the paperwork to the donor. The information is further catalogued by being entered into the archive's database where Hall officials can keep track of the individual item and also manage the consistently growing collection overall.

Once the artifact enters the Resource Centre's system, staff members begin the formal preservation process. Each item is placed into acid-free bags in order to remove any contamination that could spread and damage it as well as other pieces in the collection. Further protection includes a three-step freezing process to eliminate any organism that may have entered the item over time, particularly fabrics.

Once the preservation and conservation process is complete, the artifact is stored in the climate-controlled archives while curators decide how to publicly display the item either in the museum or as part of a travelling Outreach Program exhibit. The public presentation includes a bilingual (English and French) caption that explains the significance of the artifact to fans.

The largest hockey stick collection in the world, 4,000-plus, greets — and stops — every visitor to the Resource Centre archives.

CHAPTER 8 | HOCKEY DETECTIVES

THE GREATEST COLLECTION

Lynn Patrick receives instruction from his father, New York Rangers Head Coach Lester Patrick, no earlier than the 1934-35 NHL season at Madison Square Garden. Lester's career scrapbook *(please see page 128)* is a prized Hall artifact.

CHAPTER 9 | HOCKEY DETECTIVES

The Greatest Collection that the Hockey Hall of Fame has assembled over several decades is simply too large to publicly display each artifact. The Hall rotates both museum exhibits and outreach efforts to show as many artifacts as possible. When a piece of hockey history returns to the Resource Centre from the downtown Toronto museum or from various travels, Resource Centre staff members restart the preservation and conservation process and the item is re-entered to the archives.

Beyond the structured approach employed by the staff at the Resource Centre regarding the curation of the Hall's collection, there is a collective passion employed by the team that transcends their work. Here are the "Hockey Detectives," expressing in their own words how they safeguard the game's treasures.

PRIDE

PRICELESS COLLECTION

NAME
PHIL PRITCHARD

TITLE
Vice-President, Resource Centre & Curator
Hockey Hall of Fame

"For me, the pride in my position dates back to when I was a kid growing up loving the game of hockey. Every day, coming into work, my job is all about hockey, and the love of the job brings out all of the pride in everything that we do, whether it's setting up displays, acquiring artifacts or conducting research. I love the history of hockey, the preservation of it and the presentation of it. The passion that we have here from everyone on staff really shows in all of our displays. The pride in being part of Canada's national sport goes a long way, I'm certainly proud of it and to be working in such an establishment."

Point of Personal Pride "We pride ourselves on preservation and conservation of the artifacts so they're not just around for our lifetime but for generations from now. We want the jersey or the stick to look exactly the same 200 years from now as it does today."

From ice to ice. Before entering the collection, certain artifacts are placed in a deep freeze to eliminate potentially damaging organisms.

THE GREATEST COLLECTION

Garry Unger, long-time NHL ironman, was the focus of a classic photo that was a key clue for "Hockey Detective" Craig Campbell that led him to obtaining the photographer's hockey collection for the Hall.

PURSUIT

PRICELESS COLLECTION

NAME
CRAIG CAMPBELL

TITLE
Manager, Resource Centre & Archives
Hockey Hall of Fame

"In many cases, we'll go to an event, say, the Division 1, Group A, IIHF Men's World Championship or the Canadian Women's Hockey League All-Star Game, or the Memorial Cup and, of course, the Stanley Cup Final. Oftentimes, we'll have a display that we will use to showcase our artifacts but also to preserve the moment by collecting artifacts from the event. We also have contacts in the various federations, leagues and teams who help us by sending artifacts to include in the collection. Then there are the fans from all over the world, whether from South Africa or Saskatchewan, who will send us items that represent something of importance to them that they would like to preserve. And then we'll try to find things. For example, I will sometimes see an image that has led me to a photographer and I will reach out to ask if they would like to preserve their collection with us. Fortunately, a lot of people believe in the brand of the Hockey Hall of Fame, the museum, the logo and they want to preserve their items with us forever."

A Favourite Find "A picture from the Garry Unger (St. Louis Blues) photo files. The colours I find to be very striking, as well as the quality and sharpness of the image. The information on the back of the photo led me to Lewis Portnoy, a well-known photographer from the St. Louis area, who I contacted, and which eventually led to his hockey photo collection coming to the Hockey Hall of Fame."

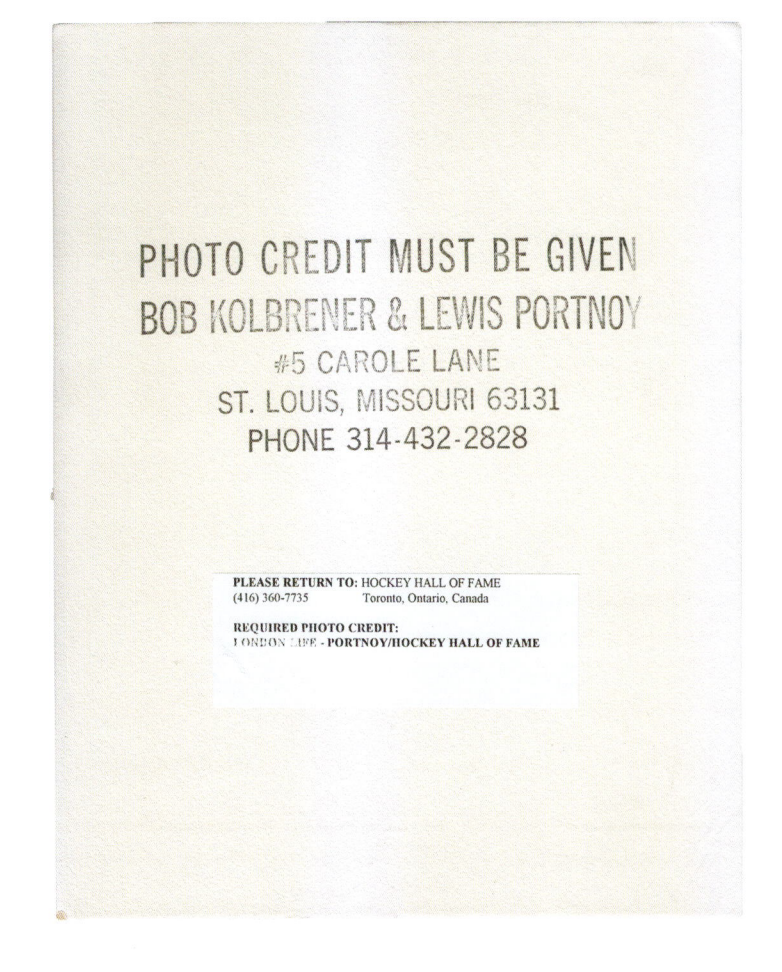

THE GREATEST COLLECTION

A vintage Black Hawks photo in the Hall's archives helped confirm the authenticity of a vintage Chicago sweater donated to the collection.

FOLLOWING LOOSE THREADS

It's called photo-matching.

Essentially, it means using an artifact from a known time and place to confirm the identity and authenticity of another suspected artifact from the same era. In the case of a sweater of hockey immortal Stan Mikita that ended up on the desk of the Resource Centre's Craig Campbell one day, it meant going into the Hall of Fame's photo archives in order to place the sweater at the same time and place of a known photograph. And it all came down to a single thread.

Campbell, at his light table and with magnifying glass in hand, scoured images of Mikita from back in the day, looking for any telltale sign that would match a photo against the physical, glorious Black Hawks red sweater that had been donated, it was assumed, by the NHL club. Turns out, one particular image of Mikita from 1964 celebrating a Hawks goal showed the stitching on the number "1" on the sleeve of Chicago's famous No. 21 had become partially unravelled. When matched against the physical sweater, the same loose stitch, in the identical location, meant that the artifact was very likely the real "MiK-Coy." Other marks and signs of wear between the image and the sweater would further confirm its identity, allowing Campbell to verify its authenticity.

CHAPTER 9 | HOCKEY DETECTIVES

Bill Hutton's 1930-31 Philadelphia Quakers (NHL) sweater arrived in the mail days after a telephone call between former Hall staffer Jeff Davis and Rod Hutton, Bill's son.

Herb Gardiner's ring from the 1923-24 championship Calgary Tigers (Western Canada Hockey League) arrived unannounced at the Hall in an envelope with no return address. It's assumed it came from the Gardiner family.

PERSON OF INTEREST

The Resource Centre's "Hockey Detectives" will probably be interested in asking you a few questions if you happen to be in possession of an artifact that would make a great addition to the Greatest Collection.

In general, they're looking to uncover items in four main areas:

1. Artifacts that players have used to establish a new milestone, while also representing different styles and eras of play and evolution.

2. Artifacts that tell the story of the individuals who have shaped the sport, such as scrapbooks, writings and equipment from families and fans. Similarly, contributions from diverse leagues and organizations that have impacted how hockey is played and enjoyed are also of interest to the Hall.

3. Random and unexpected donations that can help add a significant and new perspective to hockey history.

4. Items from fans, families, players and administrators that help preserve hockey history.

More information on artifact donation can be found by visiting the Hockey Hall of Fame's Web site: hhof.com

THE GREATEST COLLECTION

PROCESS

PRICELESS COLLECTION

NAME
IZAK WESTGATE

TITLE
Manager of Outreach Exhibits & Assistant Curator
Hockey Hall of Fame

"When something comes in, no matter how small or big, it is properly documented, we accession it, give it an ID number and preserve it in our archival facility. For materials and older woollen items, we put them through a freeze process and then enter them in the archive. We have proper humidity, temperature and climate controls that allow us to preserve the artifacts forever so they can be used for display in the museum or taken on the road to give people a chance to see them who don't have a chance to visit Toronto and the Hall of Fame itself."

Favourite Artifact "The Percy LeSueur goalie stick *(shown at right and on page 24)*. The stick is from the early 1900s and he's wood carved all of his accomplishments into it, from the Stanley Cups he won to playing in the first professional All-Star game that pre-dates the NHL. For the age of the artifact and who it belonged to, he's an Honoured Member, it's probably one of our most unique items and certainly one that I point to when I give tours. As for trophies, my favourite is probably the Canada Cup *(opposite page)*. It's a classic."

124

CHAPTER 9 | HOCKEY DETECTIVES

The Soviet team was so happy to win the Canada Cup in 1981, they wanted to bring it back in the U.S.S.R. Former Canadian Prime Minister Pierre Trudeau held firm, and the beautiful trophy remains in the Hall's collection.

125

THE GREATEST COLLECTION

WAYNE'S WORLD (HOCKEY ASSOCIATION)

Gretzky would take the professional hockey world by storm in 1978 with the Edmonton Oilers, but not before celebrating his 18th birthday at centre ice in front of thousands of his newest and closest friends.

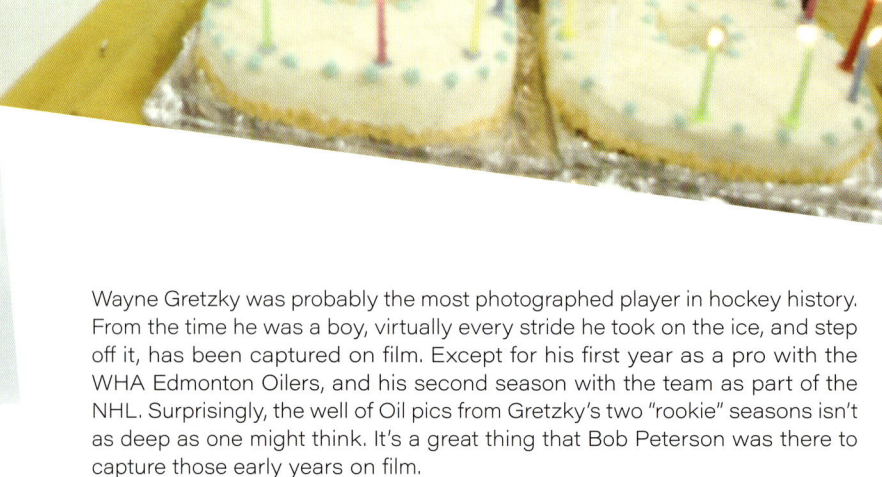

Wayne Gretzky was probably the most photographed player in hockey history. From the time he was a boy, virtually every stride he took on the ice, and step off it, has been captured on film. Except for his first year as a pro with the WHA Edmonton Oilers, and his second season with the team as part of the NHL. Surprisingly, the well of Oil pics from Gretzky's two "rookie" seasons isn't as deep as one might think. It's a great thing that Bob Peterson was there to capture those early years on film.

Among Peterson's collection of Gretzky shots is a rare image of the future superstar with his long-time idol, Gordie Howe, as part of the WHA All-Star team in 1979. Peterson's Oilers collection found its way to the Hall's archives in the summer of 2019, thanks to the work of Craig Campbell, Manager, Resource Centre and Archives, who reached out to Peterson through long-time Edmonton photo editor Tom Braid.

"In speaking with Bob, I got a real sense that he felt the Hall was the perfect destination for his collection, and saw us as a very stable and professional organization," said Campbell. "As for Tom, he was passionate about safeguarding this important part of hockey history. And now the Hall can share these photos, many of which have not been widely seen with fans everywhere."

CARNEGIE HAUL

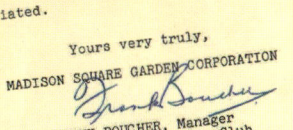

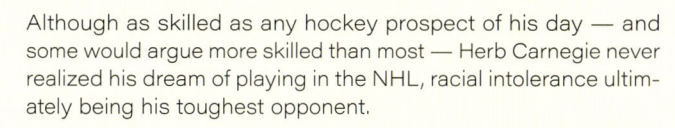

Although as skilled as any hockey prospect of his day — and some would argue more skilled than most — Herb Carnegie never realized his dream of playing in the NHL, racial intolerance ultimately being his toughest opponent.

Instead of allowing the slight to beat him down, Carnegie chose instead to meet his rejection head on with an uncommon perseverance and positivity. Following his minor league career in the 1940s and '50s — he was a prolific goal scorer who would become a teammate and personal friend of Jean Béliveau while playing with the Quebec Aces — Carnegie forged a career of philanthropy that would begin with the founding of one of Canada's first hockey schools in 1954, having schools and foundations named in his honour, and becoming a member of the Order of Canada.

In 2019, the Hall's collection was enriched with key artifacts from Carnegie's career, from photos of his earliest playing days to a letter to customs officials from the New York Rangers requesting permission for Carnegie to cross into the U.S. to attend training camp prior to the 1948-49 season.

THE GREATEST COLLECTION

128

CHAPTER 9 | HOCKEY DETECTIVES

PRESENTATION
PHIL PRITCHARD

"Everyone at the Hockey Hall of Fame has the same philosophy that we call the '3Es.' It's basically how we present everything and they are: Education, Excellence and Entertainment. When we consider an item and confirm that it meets the 3Es, we're able to present it in such a way that a fan is educated about it, it's an excellent product to view and it's also an entertaining experience. The whole preservation process revolves around this philosophy and shapes our thinking on the presentation, whether the item is in the museum, on the road for outreach or whether it's here in the Resource Centre Archives. We have to meet those three Es each and every time we look at an item. It all comes back to those 3Es."

Hall Highlight "Although we have thousands of items in our collection, for me our scrapbooks are the highlights of everything, not just because of who they belonged to, but because of why the person began collecting them in the first place, whether a family member, a player or a fan. When looking through the Hall's scrapbook collection, each and everyone has a story that comes to life and they share all the history of the game itself. My favourite is the Lester Patrick collection that goes all the way back to the early 1900s to when he was a youth, into his playing days, into his manager days, into his coaching days. The best thing is when you look at the scrapbook you can almost see Lester himself coming to life."

The Lester Patrick scrapbook is like a trip back in time — more than 100 years, in fact. It chronicles one of the game's true builders and is one of the most important artifacts in the Hall's collection.

THE GREATEST COLLECTION

PRESERVATION
CRAIG CAMPBELL

"Preservation of the artifacts is essential. We're members with various associations and we adhere to standard museum protocol when handling and caring for different objects because each object is different and requires a specific level of care. We use archival products and storage devices, temperature- and humidity-controlled rooms and security systems to ensure the safety of each artifact while here at the Resource Centre or on display at the Hockey Hall of Fame museum in downtown Toronto. When the item is on the road as part of a Legends or Outreach exhibit, for example, we always try to make sure the environment in which it's being displayed is proper, but once it's returned to this archive, we take steps to condition it before it's put back on the shelf for future use."

Legacy Work "The pride extends to all of us at the Hockey Hall of Fame in every role we play in preserving a collection that was procured by Lefty Reid, the primary curator for a number of years, and to be able to carry that legacy. Fortunately, we have great support throughout the fan world and the hockey world that allows us to do our jobs and with great pride."

PRICELESS COLLECTION

The Hockey Hall of Fame's approach to growing its collection is vast and varied. On the grassroots level, its call to community reflects the very nature of the game itself: open and unpretentious. On the professional and elite amateur levels, domestic and international, its ongoing efforts to collect and record mementoes and milestones from the sport's best represent the same excellence being pursued on the ice. The magic on the community side is that ordinary people can "enter" the Hall through a successful artifact donation and live forever alongside the game's immortals, even if only vicariously. On the elite side, the stuff that dreams are made of, the pursuit of capturing and chronicling the exploits of hockey's heroes drives imagination and grows fan bases and followings. The two rely on each other — as does *The Greatest Collection*.

"The pride extends to all of us at the Hockey Hall of Fame in every role we play in preserving a collection that was procured by Lefty Reid..."

The Resource Centre is the safe home to millions of photos and miles of film spanning the history of hockey. All of the photos featured in *The Greatest Collecton*, in fact, come via the centre's archives and its dedicated staff.

CHAPTER 9 | HOCKEY DETECTIVES

FEATURED ARTIFACT

THE MAPLE LEAF MAY HAVE BEEN HALF, BUT MARIO LEMIEUX'S EFFORT IN LEADING TEAM CANADA TO A CANADA CUP WIN IN 1987 WAS FULL.

HE LED ALL TOURNAMENT SCORERS WITH 11 GOALS, INCLUDING THE DRAMATIC GAME-WINNER IN THE FINAL AGAINST THE SOVIET UNION.

LE MAGNIFIQUE'S SWEATER IS A MAGNIFICENT PART OF THE HOCKEY HALL OF FAME'S COLLECTION.

133

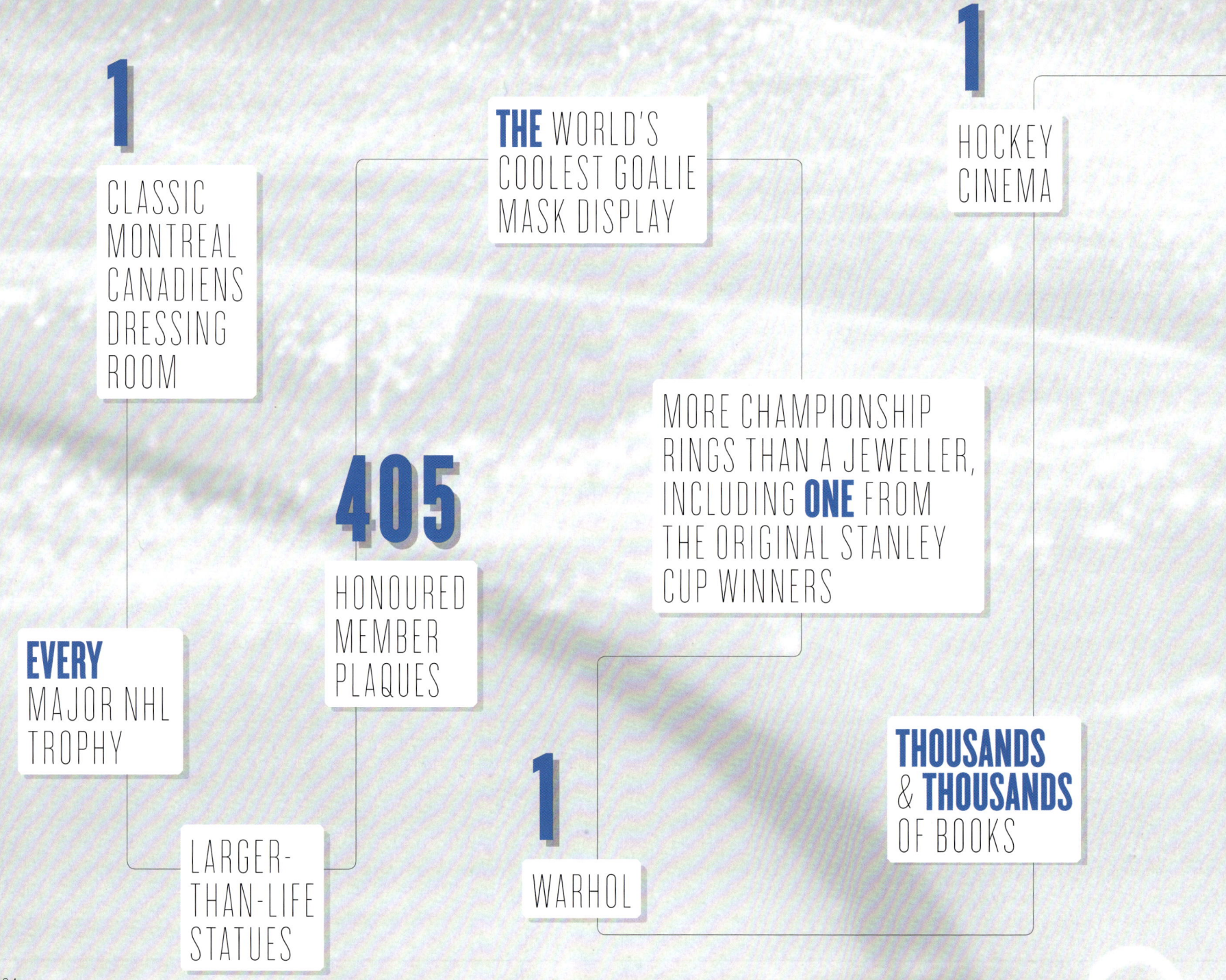

THE GREATEST COLLECTION

THE GREATEST COLLECTION

1 CLASSIC MONTREAL CANADIENS DRESSING ROOM

THE WORLD'S COOLEST GOALIE MASK DISPLAY

1 HOCKEY CINEMA

MORE CHAMPIONSHIP RINGS THAN A JEWELLER, INCLUDING **ONE** FROM THE ORIGINAL STANLEY CUP WINNERS

405 HONOURED MEMBER PLAQUES

EVERY MAJOR NHL TROPHY

LARGER-THAN-LIFE STATUES

1 WARHOL

THOUSANDS & THOUSANDS OF BOOKS

134

BY THE NUMBERS

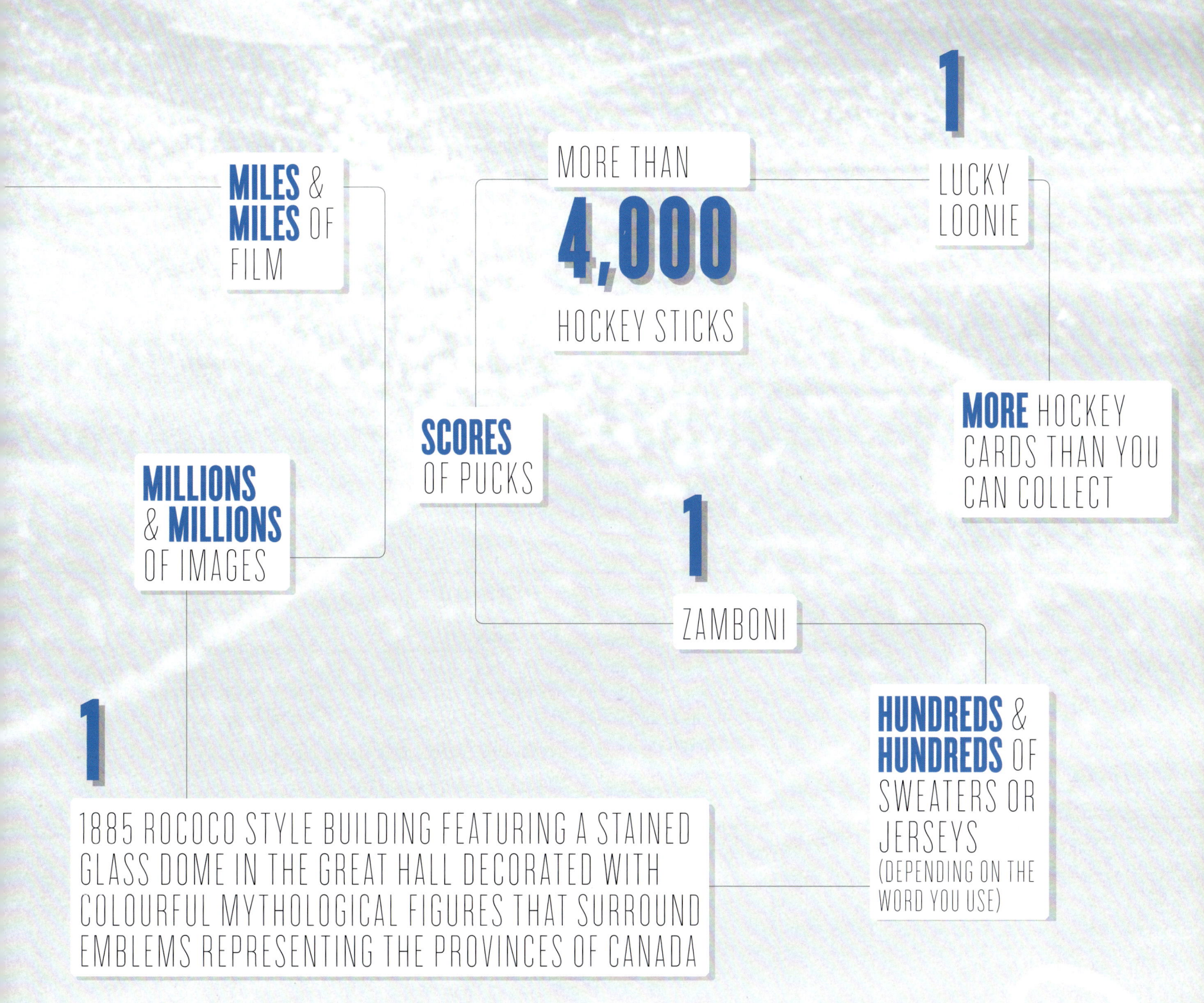

MILES & **MILES** OF FILM

MORE THAN **4,000** HOCKEY STICKS

1 LUCKY LOONIE

SCORES OF PUCKS

MILLIONS & **MILLIONS** OF IMAGES

MORE HOCKEY CARDS THAN YOU CAN COLLECT

1 ZAMBONI

1 1885 ROCOCO STYLE BUILDING FEATURING A STAINED GLASS DOME IN THE GREAT HALL DECORATED WITH COLOURFUL MYTHOLOGICAL FIGURES THAT SURROUND EMBLEMS REPRESENTING THE PROVINCES OF CANADA

HUNDREDS & **HUNDREDS** OF SWEATERS OR JERSEYS (DEPENDING ON THE WORD YOU USE)

THE GREATEST COLLECTION

TUROFSKY

ON DECEMBER 2, 1981 THE HALL RECEIVED ONE OF THE MOST IMPORTANT DONATIONS IN ITS HISTORY WHEN THE TUROFSKY COLLECTION WAS ADDED TO ITS PHOTO ARCHIVES. LOU AND NAT TUROFSKY CAPTURED THREE DECADES OF THE NHL'S 'ORIGINAL SIX' ERA (1940s-'60s), INCLUDING PLAYER PORTRAITS AND GAME ACTION. THE 19,000-IMAGE COLLECTION ALSO FEATURES THE LARGEST KNOWN QUANTITY OF HOCKEY-RELATED GLASS PLATE NEGATIVES FROM THE LATE 1920s AND '30s. HERE IS A SAMPLE OF THE BROTHERS' WORK.

The Detroit Red Wings classic sweater as seen through the Turofsky lens.

Francis "King" Clancy poses for a portrait for the first time as a member of the Toronto Maple Leafs in October of 1930 at training camp in Parry Sound, ON. Clancy was inducted into the Hockey Hall of Fame in 1958.

THE GREATEST COLLECTION

Gerry Ehman is cross-checked by Tom Johnson in front of Jacques Plante on October 19, 1960 at Maple Leaf Gardens. The Leafs beat the Montreal Canadiens 3-1.

A youthful Terry Sawchuk is shown in the Red Wings dressing room before a game against the Leafs.

HONOURED GUESTS

Ever since the Hockey Hall of Fame began operations in Toronto in the 1950s, curators and staff members have sought to build relationships with legendary hockey figures. Initially, Curators Bobby Hewitson and Lefty Reid informally wrote to Honoured Members to invite them to various Hall functions and inquire if they could assist in building the Greatest Collection. Beginning in 2009, however, the Hall instituted a program that sought to formalize the museum's relationship with its members. Now, after the Selection Committee chooses the newest class of Honoured Members, staff members travel the globe to visit the new Players, Builders and Referees in the months prior to them being enshrined, preparing them for the big event. According to Kelly Masse, the Hall's Director, Corporate and Media Relations, the Hall has four main goals that it hopes to achieve through these visits.

First, and perhaps most importantly, these meetings build a direct relationship with the new Honoured Member. Second, Hall staff review and plan the fast-paced, jam-packed and somewhat hectic nature of Induction Weekend that includes innumerable appearances, ceremonies and celebrations. Third, while no Honoured Member is obligated to provide the Hall with artifacts, staff members often travel back to Toronto with several mementoes that the Honoured Members believe are representative of their careers, which they donate to the collection. Fourth, staff will have the Honoured Member sign posters that feature the induction class, which are distributed as part of promotion efforts surrounding induction.

Individual Hall of Fame classes have reflected the museum's vision to commemorate all levels of hockey participation and competition. Indeed, even the game's greats who are best known for their professional accomplishments recognize and respect the Hall's effort to present the entire narrative of their careers. Chris Pronger, for example, donated a sweater from his high school years as well as some of his minor league sweaters. As Craig Campbell, Manager, Resource Centre and Archives explained, early artifacts from a player's minor hockey days often do not survive and stats and stories go unreported. It makes the personal visit with the Honoured Member so much more important in the telling of their entire career. Travelling the globe to meet the sport's legends provides an additional avenue for the Hall to continue building and deepening the Greatest Collection.

It's also the proper way to welcome them to a home in which they will live forever.

Chris Pronger's high school sweater from Dryden, ON.

141

THE GREATEST COLLECTION

LATEST GREATEST

The 2019 Induction Class included Jim Rutherford in the Builders category. A lifelong hockey man, Rutherford followed a 13-year NHL playing career with a successful second career in management. As general manager, he notched three Stanley Cup championships, including a pair with the Pittsburgh Penguins, the team he continued to manage at the time of induction. He won the NHL General Manager of the Year Award in 2016.

To prepare for Rutherford's induction, Hockey Hall of Fame staffers Craig Campbell and Kelly Masse visited him at his Pittsburgh office. Campbell was joined by Phil Pritchard for an earlier visit to the Rutherford family home, hosted by his sister, which garnered donations from Rutherford's youth hockey days, including a junior team photo *(goalie at left)*, and pads *(right)*.

143

BIBLIOGRAPHY

Armstrong, George. File. Doc Seaman Resource Centre.

Armstrong, John. "Hockey Resource Library and Archives." In *Hockey Hall of Fame: The Official Yearbook of the Hockey Hall of Fame*, edited by Laurie Payne, 53-75. Toronto: St. Clair Group Investments, Inc., 1993.

Bitove, Miragh. "HHOF's Resource Centre and Archives Make a Move," In *Legends: The Official Program of the Hockey Hall of Fame*, edited by Kevin Shea, 64-65.

Bucyk, John, P. File. Doc Seaman Resource Centre.

Campbell, Clarence, S. (red dot). File. Doc Seaman Resource Centre.

Diamond, Dan, and Bill Jamieson, ed. *Hockey's Heritage: 1987*. Detroit: Detroit Red Wings, 1987.

Griffith, Jeffrey. *Commemorating Greatness: the Hockey Hall of Fame's Celebration of Hockey, Canada and the Individual*. Thesis: California State University, Fullerton, 2013.

Hewitson, R.W. "Bobby," ed. *Hockey Hall of Fame Book*. Toronto: Hockey Hall of Fame, 1962

Hewitson, R.W. Bobby. File. Doc Seaman Resource Centre.

Northey, William. File. Doc Seaman Resource Centre.

O'Brien, John Ambrose. File. Doc Seaman Resource Centre.

Reid, Maurice 'Lefty'. *I Remember: Recollections of Former Hockey Hall of Fame Curator and Director, 1968-1992*. Self-published, 2015.

Roche, Bill. *The Hockey Book*. McClelland and Stewart; 1st edition 1958.

Selke, Frank J. (red dot). File. Doc Seaman Resource Centre.

Selke, Frank J. with Gordon Green. *Behind the Cheering*. Canada: McClelland and Stewart Limited, 1964.

Shea, Kevin. *The Hall: Celebrating Hockey's Heritage, Heroes and Home*. Montreal: Griffintown Media Inc., 2018.

Smith, Frank D. File. Doc Seaman Resource Centre.

Taylor, Fred 'Cyclone'. File. Doc Seaman Resource Centre.

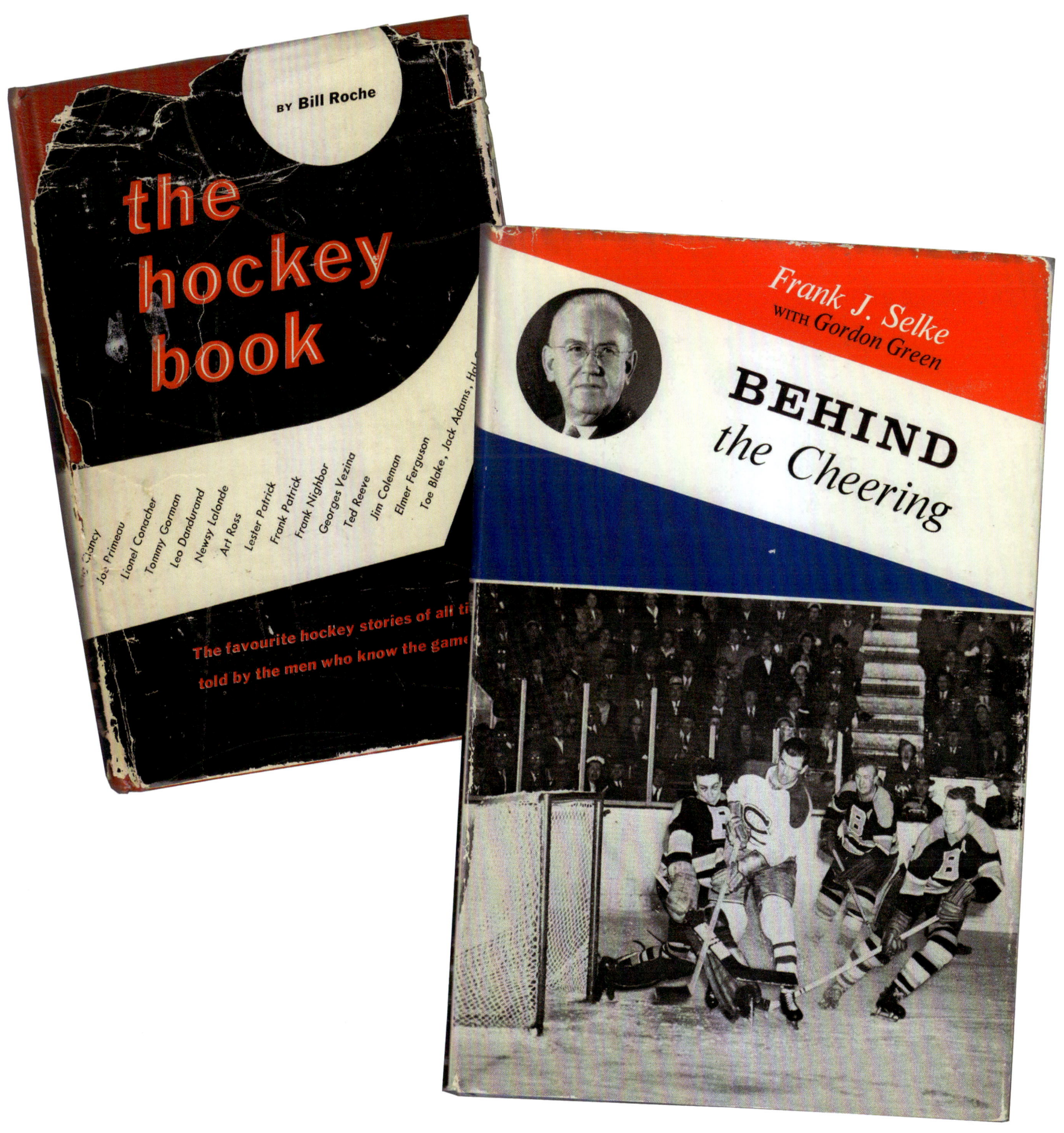

the hockey book

BY BILL ROCHE

King Clancy
Joe Primeau
Lionel Conacher
Tommy Gorman
Leo Dandurand
Newsy Lalonde
Art Ross
Lester Patrick
Frank Patrick
Frank Nighbor
Georges Vezina
Ted Reeve
Jim Coleman
Elmer Ferguson
Toe Blake, Jack Adams, Hal...

The favourite hockey stories of all ti[me]
told by the men who know the game

BEHIND the Cheering

Frank J. Selke
WITH Gordon Green

CREDITS

Covers	*Metropolitans Sweater* Jean Brosseau | HHOF	37	*Foyston Photo* HHOF
9	*Skates Photo* Derik Murray | HHOF	38	*Avco World Trophy* Matthew Manor | HHOF
11	*Taylor Hockey Stick* Matthew Manor | HHOF *Taylor Photo* HHOF *Taylor Contract* HHOF	39	*WHA Sweaters Photo* Dave Sandford | HHOF
12	*Hockey Ticket* HHOF *Pucks* Matthew Manor | HHOF *Golden Goal Display Photo* AJ Messier | HHOF	40	*Gretzky Gloves* Lisa Harmatuk | HHOF *Gretzky OMJHL Plaque* Lisa Harmatuk | HHOF *Gretzky & Howe Photo* Bob Peterson | HHOF *Howe Gloves* Matthew Manor | HHOF *Howe Puck* HHOF
13	*Ovechkin Skates* Liam Terry | HHOF *Ovechkin Photo* Paul Stinsa | HHOF *Myles Note* HHOF	41	*Broncos Jersey* Jean Brosseau | HHOF
14	*Bower Photo* Michael Burns Sr. | HHOF *Bower Chest Protector* Matthew Manor | HHOF	42	*Plante Photo* Graphic Artists | HHOF *Plante Skates* Matthew Manor | HHOF
15	*O'Brien Trophy Photo* Imperial Oil-Turofsky | HHOF	43	*Kobylyanskiy & Pritchard Photo* HHOF *Mahovlich Photo* Graphic Artists | HHOF
16	*Wanderers Team Photo* Le Studio du Hockey | HHOF	44	*Sabres Team Photo* Bob Shaver | HHOF *Hockey Ticket* HHOF *Sabre Photo* Jean Brosseau | HHOF
17	*Boon Photo* HHOF *Boon Skates* Matthew Manor | HHOF	47	*Howe Skates* Matthew Manor | HHOF
18	*Montreal Hockey Club Team Photo* HHOF *Barlow Ring* Matthew Manor | HHOF	48	*Baker Photo* HHOF
19	*Blake Frame* Matthew Manor | HHOF	49	*Rink Board Photo* Steve Poirier | HHOF *Canadian Military Photo* Le Studio du Hockey | HHOF
21	*Mosienko Letter* HHOF	50	*Goyette Jersey* Jean Brosseau | HHOF
22	*Black Hawks Display Photo* Le Studio du Hockey | HHOF	51	*Beaver Photo* HHOF *Kwong Photo* Imperial Oil-Turofsky | HHOF *Lightfoot Photo* HHOF
23	*Golden Gaels Team Photo* Le Studio du Hockey | HHOF		
24	*LeSueur Hockey Card* HHOF *LeSueur Hockey Stick* Graig Abel | HHOF	52	*Sledge Hockey Equipment* Craig Campbell | HHOF *Sledge Hockey Photo* Matthew Manor | HHOF *Wheelchair Hockey Photo* Andre Ringuette | HHOF
25	*Mikita & Hull Photo* Le Studio du Hockey | HHOF	53	*Randies Teammate Photo* Le Studio du Hockey | HHOF *Tootoo Photo* Andy Devlin | HHOF
26	*Roach Photo* HHOF *Roach Goalie Stick* Matthew Manor | HHOF	54	*RACF Squadron Sweater* Jean Brosseau | HHOF *UofT Team Photo* HHOF *Smythe Medals* Jean Brosseau | HHOF *Smythe Photo* Imperial Oil-Turofsky | HHOF
27	*Stewart Photo* James Rice | HHOF *Richard Photo* Imperial Oil-Turofsky | HHOF		
28	*200-Goal Hockey Sticks Photo* Imperial Oil-Turofsky | HHOF *Gretzky 802 Goals Photo* Matthew Manor | HHOF	55	*Shea & Pritchard Photo* HHOF *Students Photo* HHOF
29	*Apps & Selke Photo* Imperial Oil-Turofsky | HHOF	56	*Beer Case Photo* Craig Campbell | HHOF
30	*Gretzky Jersey* Craig Campbell | HHOF	57	*Szabados Jersey* HHOF *Szabados Glove & Stick* Jean Brosseau | HHOF
31	*Plante Goalie Mask* Doug MacLellan | HHOF *Hockey Ticket* HHOF *Plante Photo* Michael Burns Sr. | HHOF *Brown Photo* Portnoy | HHOF	59	*Richard Order of Canada* HHOF
32	*Trophies Photo* Matthew Manor | HHOF	60	*Dunderdale Photo* Le Studio du Hockey | HHOF
35	*Isayev Goalie Mask Photo* Andrea Leigh Cardin | HHOF	61	*Dunderdale Hockey Card* HHOF
36	*Wanderers Sweater* Matthew Manor | HHOF	62	*Gretzky Hockey Cards* HHOF

63	*Trading Cards Wrappers* HHOF		104	*Connors Disk Jacket Photo* HHOF
64	*Laviolette Hockey Card & Photo* HHOF		105	*Zamboni Photo* HHOF
65	*Joliat Cap* Dave Sandford | HHOF *Joliat Hockey Card* HHOF		106	*Upper Deck Collectors' Corner Photo* Craig Campbell | HHOF
66-73	*Hockey Cards* HHOF		107	*Walleye & Icemen Jerseys* Craig Campbell | HHOF *Wregget Goalie Mask* Matthew Manor | HHOF
74	*Pudas Hockey Card* HHOF		108	*Richard Photo* Louis Jaques | HHOF
75	*Kucherov Hockey Card* HHOF		109	*Comic Book Cover* HHOF *Playmobil Box* Jean Brosseau | HHOF *Dr. Seuss Jersey* Craig Campbell | HHOF *Gretzky Lunch Box* Lisa Harmatuk | HHOF
76	*Pucks Photo* Doug MacLellan | HHOF			
78	*CNE Pass* HHOF			
79	*NHL All-Stars vs. CCCP Photo* Paul Bereswill | HHOF *Rendez-vous Exhibit Photo* Doug MacLellan | HHOF *Venturelli Jersey* Jean Brosseau | HHOF		110	*Youngblood Goalie Masks* Steve Poirier | HHOF
			111	*The Hockey Sweater Book Cover* Craig Cambell | HHOF *Richard Hockey Sweater* Matthew Manor | HHOF
80	*Crosby Photo* Tom Dahlin | HHOF *Crosby Jersey* Hal Roth | HHOF		112	*Newman Photo* HHOF *Hanson Brothers Photo* HHOF *Ducks Jersey* Craig Campbell | HHOF
81	*HHOF Book* HHOF *Legends Program* HHOF			
82	*Reagan & Duguay Photo* HHOF *Hockey's Heritage Cover* HHOF		113	*Kariya & Gauthier Photo* Doug MacLellan | HHOF
83	*HHOF Exhibit Photo* HHOF *Smith Helmet* Matthew Manor | HHOF		115	*Salada Coins Photo* Craig Campbell | HHOF
			117	*Hockey Sticks Photo* Jean Brosseau | HHOF
84	*Exhibit Photos* HHOF		118	*Lynn & Lester Patrick Photo* Le Studio du Hockey | HHOF
85	*Exhibit Photos* HHOF		119	*Artifacts in Freezer Photo* Jean Brosseau | HHOF
86	*Plante Goalie Mask* Frank Piccolo | HHOF *Hockey Cards Mural* Frank Piccolo		120	*Unger Photo* Portnoy | HHOF
			121	*Unger Photo (back)* HHOF
87	*Beaver Sweaters, Bag & Award* Frank Piccolo | HHOF *Howe Cereal Box* Frank Piccolo | HHOF		122	*Mikita Sweater* Jean Brosseau | HHOF *Mikita Photo* Portnoy | HHOF
89	*Red Wings Sweater-Rug* Jean Brosseau | HHOF		123	*Quakers Sweater* Hal Roth | HHOF *Gardiner Ring* Craig Campbell | HHOF
90	*CCCP Sweater* Hal Roth | HHOF		124	*LeSueur Photo* HHOF
91	*CNE Display Photo* HHOF		125	*Canada Cup Photo* James Lipa | HHOF
92	*Springbok Jersey* Matthew Manor | HHOF		126	*Gretzky Photos* Bob Peterson | HHOF
93	*Selanne Pads* Mattthew Manor | HHOF *Selanne Photo* Jukka Rautio | HHOF-IIHF		127	*Carnegie Rangers Letter* HHOF *School Team Photo* Le Studio du Hockey | HHOF *Carnigie Photo* Imperial Oil-Turofsky | HHOF
94	*International Hockey Stamps* HHOF			
95	*International Hockey Cards* HHOF		128	*Patrick Scrapbook* Jean Brosseau | HHOF
96	*Great Britain Team Photo* HHOF		131	*Film Rolls Photo* Jean Brosseau | HHOF
97	*Great Britain Sweater* Hal Roth | HHOF		133	*Lemieux Sweater* Matthew Manor | HHOF
98	*Falcons Sweater* Matthew Manor | HHOF *Falcons Team Photo & Gold Medal* HHOF		134-135	*Ice Background Image* Michael Burns Sr. | HHOF
			136-139	*Turofsky Photos* Imperial Oil-Turofsky | HHOF
99	*Hockey Team Photos (Olympic)* HHOF		141	*Pronger Sweater* Craig Campbell | HHOF
100	*Road to Olympus Book Cover* HHOF		142	*Tigers Team Photo* HHOF
101	*Tarasov Photo* Imperial Oil-Turofsky | HHOF *Tretiak Photo* Graphic Artists | HHOF		143	*Rutherford Goalie Pads* Craig Campbell | HHOF
			145	*Book Covers* HHOF
103	*Edinburgh Trophy Photo* Jean Brosseau | HHOF		152	*Armstrong Photo* Graphic Artists | HHOF

ACKNOWLEDGMENTS

The Hockey Hall of Fame's collection connects to fans, guests and staff members in innumerable ways. Learning and discussing the importance of key artifacts and the overall collection has been insightful and fascinating. The goal of this book has been to share the context and historical importance of a wide array of artifacts in order to enhance the power of the item to tell hockey history.

The Hall's staff has been invaluable in this effort. Particularly, Phil Pritchard, Craig Campbell and Izak Westgate have answered numerous questions and provided unparalleled insight into how the Hall approaches building its collection. Their determination to continue the legacy of previous curators like Bobby Hewitson and Lefty Reid has not just helped frame this book, but also has left an indelible mark on the Hall's collection and outreach to those interested in hockey around the globe.

I also have appreciated working with many other staff members at the Hall. Miragh Bitove, Darren Boyko, Marco Della-Savia, Sarah Marucci, Kelly Masse, Steve Poirier, Jackie Schwartz, Dwayne Schrader, Sydney Stype, Liam Terry and Bill Wellman all provided their insight and experiences gained while working with the Hall's collection and providing a memorable experience for guests.

Years ago, I had the opportunity to spend considerable time in the Resource Centre researching and interacting with the Hall's collection while writing my master's thesis, *Commemorating Greatness: the Hockey Hall of Fame's Celebration of Hockey, Canada, and the Individual*, at California State University, Fullerton. During this time I grew to appreciate the extent of the Hall's physical and literary holdings as well as the constant communication between staff members and hockey dignitaries. These collections, and staff members' intimate knowledge of their contents, highlight a key feature of this book: the Hall regularly refreshes its exhibits since all of the material cannot be displayed at once. This constant rotation provides new experiences with each Hall visit, all of which is rooted in material that showcases hockey history.

Griffintown Media has been a fantastic partner, as their working relationship with the Hockey Hall of Fame has resulted in several key additions to the book. The designs are elegant and connect the content in the narrative to the visual beauty of the Hall's collection. Thank you to Jim McRae, Salma Belhaffaf, Katrysha Gellis and Jim Hynes.

Friends and family make hockey one of the most enjoyable sports to follow. I regularly look forward to seeing my cohorts Eli Rosu, Ryan Rajmoolie, Jason Newton and Daniel Naiman at the Sport Card Expo, and whom I first became friends with on hobby message boards like Hobby Insider. To industry shapers like Dr. Brian Price, Chris Carlin, Dianne Price, I appreciate all you have done for me personally and for the card industry as a whole.

Finally, my family and I all learned about hockey with the creation of the Mighty Ducks of Anaheim. None of this would be possible without my parents', Mike and Janett Griffith, continual dedication to attending games and for supporting my hobby that has allowed me to travel internationally, learn about hockey history and to write a book alongside the Hockey Hall of Fame.

ADDITIONAL ACKNOWLEDGEMENT
Bobby Burrell's Vintage Hockey Collector publications are a great resource for organizing the Hall's collections of hockey cards and food and beverage artifacts, some of which are featured in this book.

THE GREATEST COLLECTION

NATIONAL TREASURE SERIES

The Greatest Collection is the final book in the National Treasure Series (NTS), a three-volume set that focuses on the Hockey Hall of Fame.

THE OTHER NTS TITLES

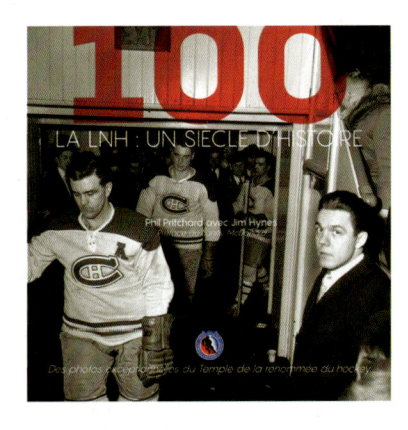

A Century of NHL Memories
Rare Photos from the Hockey Hall of Fame

French version
La LNH : un siècle d'histoire
Des photos exceptionnelles du Temple de la renommée du hockey

A Century of NHL Memories features fantastic photos snapped by legends of photojournalism, and selected for their beauty or originality, or both; these photos cast hockey's heroes in different light, take you into the heart of action or reveal as much about the charm of an era as the game on the ice. The book unveils 130 stunning images selected from the Hall's famed collection of 3 million-plus photographs, and features a special foreword by Lanny McDonald.

A limited, hand-numbered edition of the book is also available *(right)*.

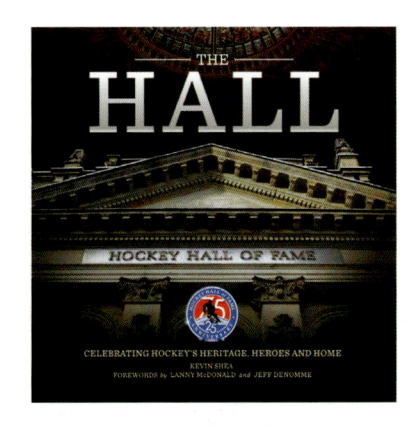

The Hall
Celebrating Hockey's Heritage, Heroes and Home

The Hall is a stunning hardcover book that commemorates the milestone 75/25 anniversary (75 years since founding/25 years in its iconic home) of the Hockey Hall of Fame. The book uncovers the Hall's fascinating history with text by award-winning author Kevin Shea, captivating photos from the Hall's famed collection and a beautiful chapter on the Stanley Cup. It also features artist-drawn portraits of all 399 Honoured Members through the 2017 induction year — for the first time ever in print!

National Treasure Series titles are sold in bookstores and online, including at nationaltreasureseries.com

100
A CENTURY OF NHL MEMORIES

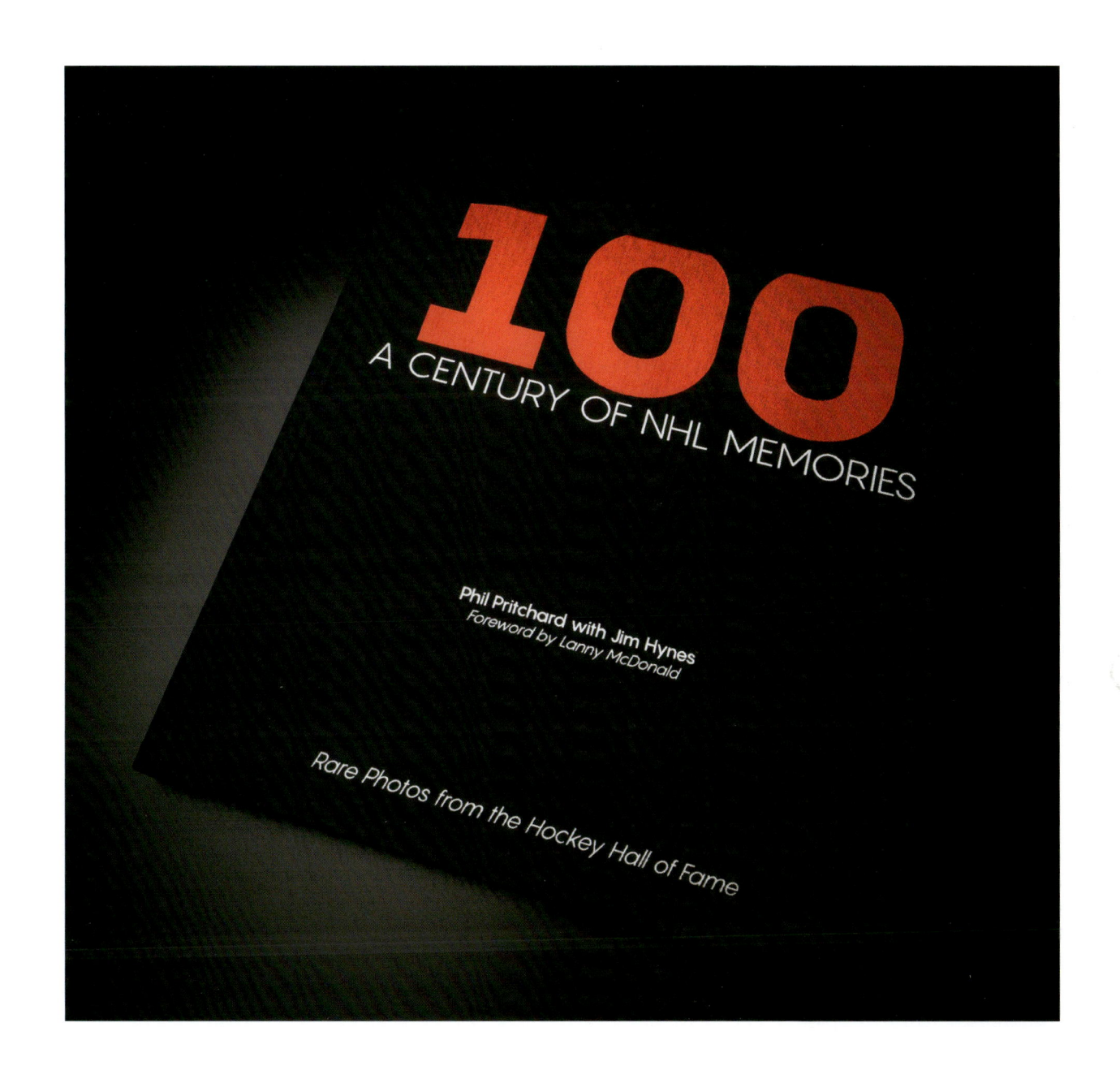

Phil Pritchard with Jim Hynes
Foreword by Lanny McDonald

Rare Photos from the Hockey Hall of Fame